Christmas A Very Peculiar History™

With lashings of second helpings

'Heap on more wood
The wind is chill
But let it whistle as it will
We'll keep our Christmas merry still.'

Scottish novelist Sir Walter Scott
(1771–1832)

To new-borns Finley and William. May they
have many Merry Christmases!

F MacD

Editor: Jamie Pitman
Artists: Mark Bergin, David Antram, Carolyn Franklin, John
James, Li Sidong, Nicholas Hewetson, iStockphoto, Fotolia

Published in Great Britain in MMX by
Book House, an imprint of
The Salariya Book Company Ltd
25 Marlborough Place, Brighton BN1 1UB
www.salariya.com
www.book-house.co.uk

ISBN-13: 978-1-907184-50-5

© The Salariya Book Company Ltd MMX

1 3 5 7 9 8 6 4 2
A CIP catalogue record for this book is available
from the British Library.
Printed and bound in Egypt.
Printed on paper from sustainable sources.

Visit our website at **www.book-house.co.uk**
or go to **www.salariya.com** for **free** electronic versions of:
You Wouldn't Want to be an Egyptian Mummy!
You Wouldn't Want to be a Roman Gladiator!
You Wouldn't Want to be a Polar Explorer!
**You Wouldn't Want to sail on a 19th-Century
Whaling Ship!**

WARNING: The Salariya Book Company accepts
no responsibility for the historical recipes in this
book. They are included only for their historical
interest and may not be suitable for modern use.

Christmas A Very Peculiar History™

With lashings of second helpings

Written by
Fiona Macdonald

Created and designed by
David Salariya

"At Christmas play and make good cheer, For Christmas comes but once a year."

English poet and farmer
Thomas Tusser (c 1524–1580)

"Yes, Virginia, there is a Santa Claus. He exists as certainly as love and generosity and devotion exists, and you know that they abound and give to your life its highest beauty and joy."

New York Sun newspaper, USA, 1897.

'Christmas is forced upon a reluctant and disgusted nation by the shopkeepers and the press; on its own merits it would wither and shrivel in the fiery breath of universal hatred.'

Anglo-Irish dramatist and activist
George Bernard Shaw (1856–1950)

Contents

Putting Christmas on the map

1. Annunciation at Nazareth
2. Wise Men travel from Persia
3. Roman ship
4. Temple at Jerusalem
5. Joseph, Mary and Jesus travel to Egypt
6. Jesus born in Bethlehem
7. Roman soldier

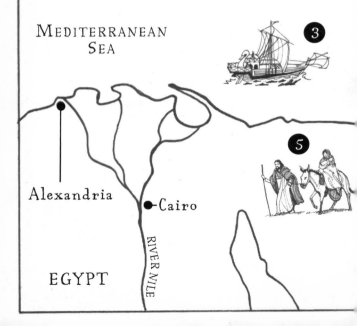

MEDITERRANEAN SEA

3

5

Alexandria

Cairo

RIVER NILE

EGYPT

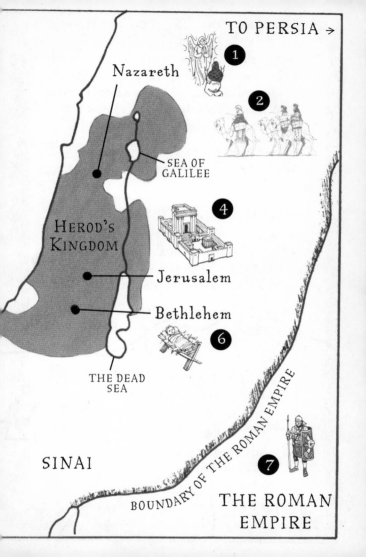

TO PERSIA →

Nazareth

SEA OF
GALILEE

HEROD'S
KINGDOM

Jerusalem

Bethlehem

THE DEAD
SEA

SINAI

BOUNDARY OF THE ROMAN EMPIRE

THE ROMAN
EMPIRE

"These poor simple creatures are made after superstitious festivals, after unholy holidays... I have known some that have preferred Christmas Day before the Lord's Day [Sunday]."

Puritan Member of Parliament, speaking about English men and women, 1644.

"Bah! Humbug!... Every idiot who goes about with 'Merry Christmas' on his lips, should be boiled with his own pudding, and buried with a stake of holly through his heart."

Ebenezer Scrooge, in Charles Dickens's story, *A Christmas Carol*, 1843.

"Go Christmas, Go Hannukah, Go Kwanzaa, Go Solstice... Go Christmas, go Hanukkah, go whatever holiday you Wannakuh!"

Advertising slogan by a major clothing retailer, USA, 2009. It was withdrawn after protests.

Introduction

Christmas! 'It's the most wonderful time of the year...' or so the 1963 hit song confidently informed listeners. The title of a later Christmas compilation album, 'What a Night!' (issued 2008), sounded rather less certain – but perhaps the double meaning was unintentional.

Assuming that Christmas IS indeed wonderful, this book will ask why so many people worldwide still feel that it is so special. It will also investigate how today's frantic festive combination of family, food and frenzied shopping – to say nothing of novelty musical numbers and mawkish movies – came to be linked to a religious ritual remembering the birth of an apparently fatherless baby to a poor, homeless refugee.

Time to give...

Why do we like Christmas? Is it just because it's a holiday – a welcome break for anything between one day and a fortnight away from the pressures of work or school? Is it – in the northern hemisphere at least – a warm and brightly-shining spot in a cold and gloomy season? Is it because of all the presents? Not just because we like getting them, but because it's also good to give – to our friends, our family and to charities. In the USA, for example, over half the donations to good causes are made in the weeks before Christmas Day.

...and to consume

Is Christmas so much fun because we enjoy the food, the drink, the decorations and the parties? Because it's nice to get Christmas cards from distant friends, and send our own Christmas greetings? Or do we like lighting candles, singing carols, watching Nativity plays and waiting for Santa Claus? Is Christmas simply a great occasion for shops and businesses to make lots of money? Or is it, as many people of faith believe, a time of hope and consolation?

Joy to the world!

Christmas has a long history – stretching back, confusingly, for centuries before baby Jesus Christ was born. The fact that it has survived so long suggests that it fills an important gap in our lives. A world without Christmas would be miserable. If Christmas did not exist, we would have to invent it!

Come with us! Turn the pages, and find out more!

Welcome Yule!

Welcome be ye that are here,
Welcome all and make good cheer;
Welcome all, another year,
Welcome Yule!

English carol, words first written
down around AD 1450

*Ho, ho, ho! Over here! Come
and climb on my sleigh! Ride
with me as we travel 5,000 years
back in time, to find out how
Christmas began.*

Midwinter madness

Brrrrr! It's the middle of winter here in the frosty northern hemisphere. Cold, dark and dangerous – the very dead of the year. The ground is frozen hard; the streams are covered with ice. There's no green grass to feed the cattle; fruits and berries have vanished from the leafless trees. Wild creatures have migrated south, or hidden themselves to hibernate. Fish don't leap in the rivers. No birds sing.

Each day, there is less light. The nights grow longer and colder. As you huddle under your smelly goatskin rug, you're hungry and shivering. Have you stored enough grain? Have you cut enough firewood? And will something fierce and nasty from the forests prowl out of the darkness to eat you?

Just as bad, the dim grey days are making you very miserable. You're tired, slow, clumsy, depressed. You feel vaguely ill, and horribly lazy.

Why this winter gloom? What's happening to your world? And why – in every way – has the Sun stopped shining?

Don't worry, my friend! Be happy! It will soon be the SOLSTICE....

Turning world

Every year, the Earth orbits the Sun, spinning on its own axis. But because the Earth is tilted as it travels, sunlight does not strike its surface evenly. Instead, the amount of light reaching places on the Earth varies from day to day. This is why days can be longer or shorter at different times of the year. The difference in daylight hours from season to season increases with distance North or South from the Equator.

The Earth's axis   The Sun

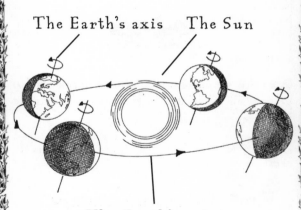

The Earth's orbit

The day the Sun stands still

Twice a year, at Midsummer and Midwinter, there are moments in time when the top and bottom of the tilting Earth get closest to, or furthest away from, the Sun. These moments are known as 'solstices'; they happen at the longest (Midsummer) and shortest (Midwinter) days.

To a person standing on the ground, the Earth's orbit and tilted angle (or 'axial tilt') make it look as if the Sun is climbing higher or sinking lower in the sky, day by day. And, at each solstice, it appears that the Sun stands still for a while, and then changes direction.

Our word 'solstice' was invented by the Romans, over 2000 years ago. Like many past peoples, they observed how the Sun seemed to stop in the sky at Midsummer and Midwinter, and gave this phenomenon a name. They combined two existing words in Latin, their language, to create a new one:

'sol' (the Sun) + 'sistere' (to stay still) = solstice!

So you see, my friend, there's no cause for despair! The Sun's not going to disappear! And after the solstice it will soon shine more strongly again. The days will get longer, the weather will grow warmer. The world will be reborn, believe me!

If you want further proof, you can visit monuments based on careful observations of the solstices. They'll show you how the Sun always rises, even at the darkest time of the year.

At Newgrange tomb in Ireland, constructed around 3,200 BC, there is a chamber built to catch a beam of light on the Winter Solstice. The sunbeam illuminates the floor of the chamber for 17 minutes before disappearing until next year.

Still not convinced? Then what what you need is light, warmth – and action. They will make you more cheerful!

Build a big bonfire!(see page 26) Hold a huge feast (see page 105) Or be like the the Romans, and throw a splendid party to celebrate the solstice!

I LOVE a party!
Hop back on to my sleigh. We're
off to Ancient Rome!

Ancient Romans celebrating
the feast of Saturnalia

SENATOR M CORNELIUS GALBA

REQUESTS THE PLEASURE OF YOUR
COMPANY AT A PUBLIC, ALL-NIGHT,
LAMP-LIT FEAST FOR

SATURNALIA

(17 – 19 DECEMBER)

- OPEN TO ALL!
- HOUSE, TABLES AND COUCHES WILL BE DECORATED WITH EVERGREEN LEAVES.
- STARTS AFTER OFFERINGS AT SATURN'S TEMPLE (THAT'S DECORATED, TOO!)
- FOLLOWED BY DANCING IN DISGUISE THROUGH THE STREETS – IF YOU DARE!

PLEASE BRING A PRESENT:

FRUIT, WINE, CANDLES AND INCENSE ARE
ALL MOST ACCEPTABLE.
GUESTS PLANNING TO PRAY AT SATURN'S
TEMPLE SHOULD BRING A WAX DOLL OR CLAY
MASK AS WELL.

REMEMBER!

SLAVES WILL BE RECLINING AT SOME TABLES, WITH
THEIR MASTERS SERVING THEM.
THAT'S THE TRADITION!
YOU HAVE BEEN WARNED...

DRESS: CASUAL. POINTED PARTY HATS.

New life

Saturn was an ancient Roman god of seeds and fertility. In mild southern Italy, where the Romans lived, the weeks after the winter solstice were a good time to start clearing fields and planting crops destined to ripen in late spring, before the hot, dry Italian summer. So they asked Saturn to help them.

First, they untied the woollen ropes that bound the feet of Saturn's statue for most of the year. This set the god's power free! Next, they offered him human sacrifices. Giving live flesh and blood was the best way early peoples knew of asking the gods to send new life to their communities, in return. But at some time – no-one knows precisely when – human bodies were replaced by wax dolls or clay masks. These became favourite gifts among Saturnalia revellers.

Peace and goodwill

Saturnalia fell at a crucial turning point in the year, when the Sun seemed to stop failing and fading, and started to grow strong again. It was a time of relief and reassurance, hope, peace and goodwill – the Sun was going to shine! It was also a time of role-reversal and fresh new beginnings. That's why masters and slaves changed places – for a while. In many Roman households, slaves and servants were set free for the whole Saturnalia festival (which eventually lasted a week, until 24 December), while their masters performed their tasks or waited on them.

Other Roman traditions, such as formal dress in public and sober good order in the streets, were also relaxed at Saturnalia. Public gambling games were allowed then (normally they were frowned upon); businesses, shops, schools and law-courts were all closed; even the army – on which Rome relied to guard its mighty empire – was mostly off-duty.

Party-pooper?

Roman writer Pliny the Younger (AD c 62-113) did not enjoy Saturnalia. In fact, he disliked it so much that he had a special soundproof room built, where he could hide away from the rest of his noisy household while they were celebrating.

The dying Sun

"In Greece and lands to the east they tell the story of Adonis [a handsome Sun-god] who was killed by a wild boar. That animal is a symbol of Winter, because a boar is a rough and brutal creature, that loves damp, muddy and frost-covered places, and feeds on acorns, which are a winter crop. This [story] is a way of saying that Winter wounds the Sun, for in Winter, we find the Sun's heat and light failing, in the same way that strength and energy fade away from all creatures at death...."

Roman writer Macrobius, around AD 400.

from Macrobius, Saturnalia book I, chapt 21.

Seen enough of Rome?
Played too many party games?
Then hop on my sleigh again.
We're heading north!

Slaughter-night

In Scandinavia, Germany and lands such as the British Isles, where Nordic and German people settled, the midwinter festival was called 'Yule'. Eating, drinking, singing, joking and story-telling lasted for 12 days. Everyone had a good time – some Viking kings made feasting compulsory – but Yuletide had grim origins. Traditionally, it began with a 'slaughter-night', in mid-December.

"It was an old custom, that when there was to be sacrifice all the bondes [farmers] should come to the spot where the temple stood and bring with them all that they required while the festival of the sacrifice lasted. To this festival all the men brought ale with them; and all kinds of cattle, as well as horses, were slaughtered, and all the blood that came from them... [was sprinkled over]... the whole of the altars and the temple walls, both outside and inside... and also the people were sprinkled with the blood; but the flesh was boiled into savoury meat for those present. The fire was in the middle of the floor of the temple, and over it hung the kettles, and the full goblets were handed across the fire; and he who made the feast, and was a chief, blessed the full goblets, and all the meat of the sacrifice..."

Snorri Sturluston, 'Heimskringla: History of the Kings of Norway' c AD 1220.

Viking celebrations

Until the 20th century, the islanders of Orkney (settled by Vikings from Scandinavia around AD 900) celebrated 17 December as 'Sow night', by killing a pig and feasting on it.

At Yule, we always drink four toasts! So raise your beakers to:

- Wise and mighty god Odin, who sends victory and power to kings! *Gulp!*

- Generous god Njord and gracious goddess Freyja, who send peace and good harvests! *Gulp!*

- To me and my kingdom! May you all be brave and loyal followers! *Gulp!*

- Last but not least, to Departed Friends! Yule is the time of year when we always remember our dead – and sometimes we see them too, riding in a ghostly Wild Hunt across the sky. *Gulp!*

Yule Log:
Celebration and sacrifice

After 'sacrifice night' and away from bloody temples, the rest of Yule was much jollier. There were feasts (of course), and also, always, a blazing wood fire. Known in Britian as a Yule Log, this special timber was not just a relic of Scandinavian customs, but was also celebrated in many other European lands. Burning it is one ancient midwinter tradition that has survived for thousands of years, right up until today.

The Yule-clog is a great log of wood, sometimes the root of a tree, brought into the house with great ceremony… laid in the fireplace, and lighted with the brand [branch or stick] of last year's clog. While it lasted there was great drinking, singing and telling of tales. Sometimes it was accompanied by… candles, but in the cottages the only light was from the ruddy blaze of the great wood fire.

Washington Irving (a traveller from the USA, writing about England in 1820)

Phew! Puff! Pant! I'm not as young as I was! Each year, this Yule Log seems to get heavier and heavier!

Still, I know my duty! Winter revellers rely on me to bring them a splendid bit of firewood — in fact, a whole tree if possible!

Right now, it seems I've struck lucky. The men of the village are doing my job for me!

People collecting a Yule Log, from *Chambers Book of Days* (1832)

Midwinter mystery?

What's so special about a big blaze at midwinter? In the past, when there was no electricity and no central heating, it would surely have been strange if there were NOT a good fire then, unless a family was desperately poor. And why surround a block of firewood with ceremonies and superstitions? Why decorate it with ribbons and greenery – or, as in some places – draw pictures on it? And why give it a name? The Yule Log is a bit of a mystery!

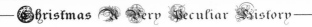

England: We drape the Yule Log with evergreen wreaths, and sprinkle it with grain and cider. If the Yule Log's too big for our cottage, we burn one end in our fireplace, and let the rest stick out through the door!

Balkans: We wrap it in silk, and offer it wine.

Southern France: We sing to it, and ask it to bless our farm. We have to carry it round our house three times before we can burn it.

Scotland (and Cornwall): We draw a face or human figure on it. If we can't find a big tree, we burn a bundle of ash twigs or birch bark.

Northern Spain (Catalonia): We keep it warm in a blanket, and feed it on grass.

Bulgaria: We ask the Yule Log tree to forgive us before we cut it down, and carry it home very gently. It must not touch the ground!

Scandinavia: Yes, we too light a big fire, and we also make promises to last all year – the first New Year's resolutions!

*Ho, ho, ho! There are at least three —
no, four — reasons why the Yule Log is
so special. All (or none) may be true.
Not even I know for sure!*

- The Yule Log is midwinter magic. The heat
  and bright glow of its flames mimic the light
  and warmth of the Sun, and encourage them
  to come back to Earth at the darkest time of
  the year. And lighting the Log with wood
  from last years's Yule fire links past, present
  and future.

- Trees are the tallest, longest-living, natural
  obects. Perhaps the gods live there? Or
  perhaps trees have god-like powers? Bringing
  one into your home will surely protect and
  bless it.

- Winter is dark and dangerous. Cold, hunger,
  even starvation, are never far away. How to
  get rid of them? Think of them as a nasty,
  ghostly old woman (in Scotland called the
  Cailleach Nolliag (Christmas Hag) – and get
  rid of her by burning her as a log!

- Give the gods a gift to ask them to send light
  and life for the coming year. The best possible
  present is a fine young man, killed in a
  sinister sacrifice. But a Yule Log, with his
  picture on it, is far less bloody.

Finding, cutting and dragging home a Yule Log – even if I help you! – takes a great deal of time and trouble. Why did past people bother? Was it worth it?

Well, we thought so!
Because...

- While a Yule Log burned, our houses were safe from witchcraft or the devil.

- Wood from last year's Log was a lucky charm. It stopped us being struck by lightning, and also kept hailstorms away.

- Yule Log ashes, sprinkled on cattle, protected them from pests. Ashes also made our fields more fertile.

- Sparks from the Yule Log carried lucky wishes.

- A plough made from left-over Yule Log wood made our crops grow better.

- And we loved the feasting and drinking that went on for as long as the Yule Log kept burning!

TV tradition

Strange but true. One of the most popular US Christmas TV broadcasts is a three-hour film – of a fireplace! This is not, however, an ordinary, everyday chimney. It stands in the home of New York's Lord Mayor, is hung with Christmas stockings, and has a Yule Log burning brightly on the hearth.

First broadcast in 1966, the original film wore out after just four years. The current version was made in 1970. A six minute shot of flickering flames, it repeats on an endless loop, backed by a soundtrack of seasonal songs.

Thinking that viewers might find the film old-fashioned, broadcasters axed the Yule Log show in 1989. But, perhaps as a comforting gesture after the shock of 9/11, they brought it back for Christmas 2001. Today, the Yule Log crackles and sparks not only on TV, but has a website[1] and a podcast, as well. It's even been remade for a rival HD channel – where it shows for 24 hours, from dawn on Christmas Day.

1. http://www.theyulelog.com/

Burn your Yule Log, or eat it?

Around 1870, a French patissier (expert cake-maker) decided to invent a new dessert to replace the traditional fruit cakes usually eaten at Christmas Eve feasts. He called it 'Bûche de Noel' (Christmas Log). Made of rich yellow sponge, spread with chocolate filling, and rolled up to look like a log, it was decorated with brown buttercream and chocolate shavings then topped with tiny meringues shaped like mushrooms.

Like to make a Bûche de Noel, but think it sounds too difficult? Relax! Enjoy yourself! And try the simple recipe overleaf!

It's just as rich and fattening – and delicious – as Bûche de Noel, but much quicker and easier. And it 'cooks' in the wintry ice and snow – or (better and safer) in a refrigerator.

Yummy orange Yule Log

You will need:

- One packet (about 15) Ginger Nut biscuits.
- 400 g (approx) tinned mandarin orange segments in natural juice
- 227 ml (1/2 pt) double cream
- 60 ml (4 level tablespoons) icing sugar
- 60 ml (4 level tablespoons) unsweetened cocoa powder
- A little extra icing sugar, for decoration
- An electric whisk or hand whisk

1. Stir the icing sugar and cocoa together to get rid of any lumps.
2. Drain the juice from the orange segments into a small bowl.
3. Pour the cream into a big bowl. Whisk until it just begins to thicken. Gently stir in the icing sugar and cocoa. Go on whisking until the cream is very thick.
4. One at at time, dip each biscuit quickly into the orange juice (don't let it get too soggy!), then spread one side with cream. Stand the creamy biscuits upright, side by side, on a serving dish, sticking them together to make a 'log' shape. Add one or two orange segments in between each biscuit, as you go along. You should aim to use about half the cream.

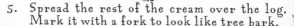

5. Spread the rest of the cream over the log. Mark it with a fork to look like tree bark.
6. Sprinkle a little icing sugar over the log (to look like snow!). If there are any orange segments left, use them to decorate the log as well.
7. Chill the log in the fridge – NOT outside in the snow! – for 4-6 hours minimum.

Doubly delicious! That recipe features TWO midwinter traditions: Yule Logs — and oranges.

Golden globes

Small, sharp-tasting, sweet-smelling, and glowing bright in dark December, mandarins, clementines and tangerines are all known as 'Christmas oranges'. Why? In the northern hemisphere, they are at their best and ripest around midwinter. And traditionally they are gifts at festival times.

In Europe and North America, little oranges were a fruity treat, tucked into the toes of children's Christmas stockings. In China (where oranges first grew), they were symbols of plenty and good fortune, and are still given to friends at New Year.[1]

---

1. *Chinese New Year usually falls in February in the Western calendar.*

Ancient magic things to do at midwinter

- **Austria and the Alps: Get chased by a Krampus!**

These fearsome monsters have wild shaggy coats, big sharp teeth, huge long horns, and terrible sharp claws (that's what their name means). They are ancient evil spirits that appear around midwinter. They'll chase you with chains and bells. Some people say it's lucky if they catch you.

Perchetn (followers of the shining goddess Perchta) are similar monsters, but female. They represent dead souls.

- **Iceland: Swear at (or rather, over) a boar!**

Join hands and make a solemn promise, then sacrifice the poor creature. Yule is the traditional time for swearing oaths.

- **Germany: Roll huge blazing wheels downhill!**

Wheee! That will encourage the midwinter Sun.

- **Germany (again): make cakes for Hertha!**

  She's the kindly, welcoming goddess of hearth and home, which are extra important in cold winter time. Traditionally, the cakes are shaped like cosy fireside slippers, but Hertha's not fussy.

- **Russia: Sing songs to Kolyada**

  Who? She's the ancient Sun-goddess. Please her, and she'll make the Sun shine.

- **Balkans: Dance, and light bonfires!**

  Dancing honours the dying winter Sun; the fires keep visiting dead souls warm.

- **Finland: Smear your doorposts with butter!**

  This will feed Beiwe, the Sun-goddess, and give her strength to keep travelling across the sky.

- **Greece: Wrap newborn babies in garlic, or singe their toenails. (NEVER, NEVER, NEVER try this yourself!)**

  Both will stop babies born at midwinter from turning into vampires!

🎵 Long time ago, in Bethlehem
So the Holy Bible say,
Mary's boy child Jesus Christ
Was born on Christmas Day. 🎵

Christmas song, written by African-American
composer Jester Hairston in 1956.

*That's a lovely song, and it tells
an amazing story. But wait —
let's sing it again, and listen a
little bit more closely. There's
rather a lot that the song doesn't
tell us! How long ago? Why Bethlehem? Who was
Mary? And how did her son give his name to the
world's biggest, best-known, holiday season? Let me
help you find out more!*

Chapter Two

Long time ago, in Bethlehem

There are no eye-witness accounts or government documents recording the birth of Jesus. As the song says, we only learn about it from the Bible, where it is described not once, but twice — and in two different versions! It appears in gospels — stories with a religious message — written by Matthew and Luke.

Turn over the page, and you can compare what they say.

Gospel story 1: According to Matthew

- Mary was a Jewish girl engaged to a Jewish man named Joseph. She found that she was to have a child "from the Holy Spirit"[1]

- Joseph was not the baby's father. He feared public disgrace and decided to end the engagement. But before he could do this, he had a dream. In it, an angel told him to marry Mary, adopt the baby, and name it Jesus.

- After baby Jesus was born, Wise Men from the East followed a bright star westwards. They believed it would lead them to a new king of the Jews.

- At Jerusalem, the Wise Men met Jewish King Herod. He was shocked, scared – and very angry – to hear their story.

- The Wise Men travelled to Bethlehem and gave royal gifts to Jesus (see page 136). After a dream warning them not to go back to Herod, they left for home straight away.

- Furious, Herod gave orders to kill all babies under two years old in Bethlehem.

- To save Jesus, Mary and Joseph fled, as refugees, to Egypt.

1. The words in quotation marks are from the Bible.

Gospel story 2
According to Luke

- Mary was a young girl living in Nazareth. An angel appeared and told her she had "found favour with God". By the power of God's Holy Spirit, she would have a son.

- Mary praised God, and thanked him for choosing a "lowly" person (herself) for such an important task.

- Roman Emperor Augustus ordered a census (population count). For this, Mary and Joseph travelled from Nazareth to Joseph's home town, Bethlehem.

- At Bethlehem, there was "no room at the inn". Mary gave birth to a baby boy, and laid him in a manger (feeding place for cattle).

- The same night, an angel appeared to shepherds in fields outside Bethlehem, and announced that "a Saviour, who is the Messiah" was born. More angels appeared, praising God and singing "Peace on Earth among men with whom God is pleased". The shepherds hurried to see baby Jesus.

- At eight days old, Jesus was taken to the Jewish Temple at Jerusalem. When they saw him there, two elderly Jewish prophets praised God for sending a Saviour. Then Mary and Joseph took Jesus to Nazareth.

Which of those gospel stories is correct? No-one knows for sure. Perhaps both tell different parts of the same true story. Or perhaps the writers are not aiming to tell us 'what really happened', but are trying to show us how important they believed baby Jesus's birth was.

Gospel facts and figures

- **What?** Life-stories of Jesus, by early Christian teachers.

- **How many?** Four (authors: Matthew, Mark, Luke and John). Only two tell of the birth of Jesus.

- **When?** Written between around AD 65 and 100. This was after eye-witnesses to Jesus's birth had died.

- **How created?** By blending word-of-mouth memories of Jesus's life with ancient Jewish prophecies, and, perhaps, fragments of earlier texts (now lost).

- **Why?** To spread a new faith, Christianity, and win new believers. Also, to claim that Jesus was the Messiah, a holy king foretold in ancient Jewish prophecies.

People and places

Bethlehem: Birthplace of King David (lived around 900 BC), one of the greatest Jewish leaders. Jesus's adoptive father, Joseph, was descended from him. Ruled by Rome, helped by a Jewish king, Herod.

The Messiah: Jewish people hoped for a Messiah: a king from David's tribe, specially chosen by God. He would free the Jews from suffering, injustice (and Roman rule) and lead them to a better future.

Jesus Christ: Was baby Jesus born to be the Messiah? Matthew's angels said so! Matthew also named Jesus 'Christos' (Chosen One, in Greek). Today, Christians call him 'Jesus Christ'.

Jewish people joined in many rebellions against Rome. According to Roman historian Josephus, these were led not by a Messiah, but by 'imposters and deceivers' promising 'marvels and signs'.

Questions, questions

Many Christians believe that the gospels describe real-life events, and that Jesus – 'Mary's boy child' Jesus Christ – was born the Son of God. They honour his birthday as a special holy day – the second most important in their whole religious year, after Easter.

Other people – Christians *and* non-Christians – see the gospel accounts of Jesus's birth as an inspiring, thought-provoking, but mostly imaginary story.

Glorious myth or genuine history? A few gospel passages still leave readers puzzling.

Test your brain power! How would you solve the following problems? Suggested answers are printed upside down.

• **Different dates**

Roman writers recorded the years of King Herod's reign (40–4 BC), and the date of the census that sent Mary and Joseph to Bethlehem (AD 6). These dates do not match details in the gospel stories. So when was Jesus born?

Probably, towards the end of Herod's reign, no later than 4 BC. Luke's gospel may be confusing the census of AD 6 – which caused famous anti-Roman riots – with an earlier, quieter, one.

• **Horrid history?**

There is no mention anywhere, apart from Matthew's gospel, of Herod's mass-murder at Bethlehem. How could such a major tragedy have disappeared from history? Did the massacre actually happen?

Probably not. But Herod was a murderer! A very successful king, he was a most unhappy husband. He married ten wives, who all plotted behind his back to get power for their sons. He had his second wife, her mother and his brother-in-law killed; they were dangerous rivals.

• **Translation troubles?**

An ancient Jewish prophecy foretold that a young woman would have a son who would save the Jewish people. Matthew repeated this prophecy, claiming that Jesus was that son, but changed 'young woman' into 'virgin'. Biologically, virgin birth is not normally possible. Was Matthew making a mistake?

Matthew chose his words deliberately. Like other early Christians, he believed in miracles. Today, some people do; others don't.

• Suspicious star?

Many ancient peoples, from Babylon to India and China, were keen star-gazers. Yet none of their observations record a new, bright star shining in the Western sky around 4 BC. Did the Wise Men (probably astrologers from Iran) imagine the star? Or was their star-story invented by the gospel-writer?

The search for the star continues. Just possibly, it was two planets, Saturn and Jupiter, shining close together in 7 or 6 BC.

Your're forgetting a very important part of the gospel story! What about us? Angels, glorious angels, soaring and swooping in the sky. We're messengers from God, linking humans with heaven. And we sing – divinely – as we dance among the stars!

FLYING TONIGHT? LOOK OUT!

ANGEL ALERT

* AWESOME and AMAZING *
* WINGED and WONDROUS *
* SWIFT, SHINING SPIRITS *

A HANDY GUIDE TO ANGEL-SPOTTING

Angels come in nine ranks, which are then divided into three heirarchies, according to how close to God they are:

Highest
Seraphim, Cherubim, Thrones

Middle
Dominions, Virtues, Powers

Lowest
Principalities, Archangels, Angels

BUT BEWARE THE FALLEN, REBELLIOUS ANGEL 'LUCIFER'!

Holy Land heritage

Thanks to travelling preachers and gospel-writers like Matthew and Luke, the Christian faith spread throughout the Roman Empire and beyond, from Britain to the borders of China. By around AD 200, Christians living far away began to travel on pilgrimage to the place where Jesus had been born, lived, and died. They called it the Holy Land.

In Bethlehem the cave is pointed out where He [Jesus] was born, and the manger in the cave where He was wrapped in swaddling clothes.[1] And the rumour is in those places, and among foreigners of the Faith, that indeed Jesus was born in this cave who is worshipped and reverenced by the Christians.

Christian scholar Origen of Alexandria (Egypt), lived c AD 185–254.

1. Strips of cloth

In AD 637, the Holy Land was conquered by Muslim armies. For many years, Christian pilgrims continued to visit it peacefully, but by AD 1096, Christians and Muslims were at war, fighting the first of many Crusades (religious wars). Both sides – and the Jews – claimed the right to rule the holy city of Jerusalem, plus the surrounding land. Tragically, peace and goodwill, as offered by the gospel angels, have rarely returned since then to the land where Jesus was born.

Did you know? The Muslim holy book, the Qur'an, also tells the story of Jesus's birth. As in the gospel version, an angel appears to Maryam (Mary) with a message from Allah (God): she will receive "the gift of a holy son".

Like Mary in the gospel, Maryam also gives birth away from home and safety, this time, under a palm tree. At first, Maryam's family is shocked, but the baby Isa (Jesus) rebukes them: "I am indeed a servant of Allah: He hath given me revelation and made me a prophet."

"God rest you merry, gentlemen,
Let nothing you dismay.
For Jesus Christ our Saviour,
Was born on Christmas Day..."

Christmas carol from England.

Old & new

Putting the 'Christ' into 'Christmas'

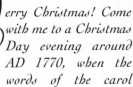

Merry Christmas! Come with me to a Christmas Day evening around AD 1770, when the words of the carol opposite were written. Those carol-singers think that Jesus was born around midwinter – on 25 December, to be precise. They spent last night eating and drinking around a Yule Log fire, they've decorated their homes with branches, and they hope for presents from the rich gentlemen (and their wives) who they are currently serenading. This morning, they went to to Church, and right now they're singing songs about baby Jesus. For them, Christmas is a happy mixture of ancient pagan tradition and Christianity.

*But how did this mixing happen?
How did such an important
religious festival come to be
celebrated on – or very close to –
the winter solstice? Who put the 'Christ' into
Christmas? Let's investigate!*

Remember the gospels in Chapter 2? They're the most important source of information about Jesus – and they tell us almost nothing about his birth date! In fact, they suggest that it WASN'T at the winter solstice. Luke's shepherds and their sheep would probably have been sheltering in a cave on the coldest, darkest, nights of the year, rather than risking their lives out in the open fields – there were many wolves!

Like the gospel-writers, early Christian scholars around AD 100–200, did not know the day when Jesus had been born. But this did not stop them trying to find out, by making amazingly complicated calculations.

When's your Christmas Day?

 Tertullian

18 January... or February

 Clement of Alexandria

18 November or 20 May

 Eastern Christian

We don't worry about birthdays. We celebrate Jesus's baptism instead – on 6 January!

 Computist

28 March

 Hippolytus of Rome

2 April

 Origen

It's wrong to celebrate Jesus's birthday...

That's how the pagans honour their gods!

When, oh when?

Today, our lives can be timed – and recorded and controlled – down to the last split-second. But for most of the past, most people did not know precisely what date or time it was. They also had no idea of exactly when they themselves had been born, especially if they were poor or unimportant.

Scholars and scribes did measure time and compile calendars. But Roman, Jewish, Greek, Egyptian and other national calendars were all very different and did not agree. Some measured time by the Sun, some by the Moon, some by Olympic sports festivals. Some dated days from nightfall; others from midnight or dawn. Many marked the passing years by keeping lists of kings; others counted from the date they thought the world began. To increase the difficulty, very few ordinary people could read or write, so dates could easily be confused or forgotten.

In AD 354, a wealthy Christian called Valentius of Rome bought himself a wonderful present. What was it? A book! Not just any old text, but a very special volume: hand-written, beautifully bound – and the first ever (that we know of) to have full-page pictures.

Lucky Valentius!
I hope he enjoyed them!

It's official!

Valentius's book also contained a list of important Roman religious festivals. And, guess what! Towards the end of the list, he could read this entry: "25 December, Christ born in Bethlehem, Jewish kingdom."

Is Christmas Day African?

Here's something more! Another piece of evidence! In AD 400, Church scholars in Rome clashed with a group of rebel Christians. This was their reason: the rebels refused to change their way of worshipping. It had begun in North Africa around AD 312, and included honouring 25 December as Jesus's birthday. Did the African rebels invent this festival, or were they copying others before them? We do not know. But why did anyone choose to celebrate Jesus's birth that day, after earlier Church scholars had suggested so many other dates?

Christmas Old and new

Christians took over an ancient Roman holiday, the Feast of the Undying Sun, and made it their own. It fell on the day when pagan Romans celebrated the winter solstice: 25 December.

Old scholar

NO! That's wrong! Early Christians hated Roman festivals, and would not join in with them.

Modern scholar

Instead, they copied an ancient Jewish tradition. This taught that holy people (such as Jewish prophets) lived 'whole' lives; that is, they were conceived (or born) and died on the same day of the year. Christians claimed that Jesus died on 25 March or 6 April because...

Stop! No more explanations! My head is spinning already!

Stay cool! Keep calm! Just believe me when I say that Christians thought that Jesus had died on either 25 March or (less likely) 6 April, and been conceived on the same date. Since pregnancy lasts nine months, that meant he must have been born on 25 December or (less likely) on 6 January!

Modern scholar

Phew! That's complicated! I'm going out for a little fly around. I need some fresh air!

58

Christ's-Mass?

The most important Western church service was called 'Mass'. The name comes from its closing words: 'Go! It is finished!'. In Latin, the language spoken by West-European priests until the AD 1500s, this was: 'Ite! Missa est!'.

Of course, the Mass held on 25 December was soon named after Jesus Christ. And, before long, the church service gave its name to the whole holy day (holiday). In England, the earliest recorded use of the day-name 'Christes Maesse' is dated 1038. That makes it one of the oldest words in the English language.

Midnight Mass

The first Mass of Christmas was always held at the very beginning of the day: midnight! Today, Midnight Mass marks the start of holiday celebrations for millions of Christians – and for many, many more non-believers. They go to church to enjoy candlelight and carols, and to feel close to their family. Now, over 2000 years after Jesus was born, Midnight Mass has become a cherished midwinter tradition.

X-Mass

No, this is not a lazy, disrespectful way of writing 'Christmas'. No, it is not a modern invention, to avoid using the religious name, 'Christ', at a multicultural holiday. Instead, it is code – in early Greek, the language of the gospels!

In the Greek alphabet, the first three letters of 'Christ' are written 'X' (Chi) and 'P' (Rho). Together, these became a holy symbol for the very first Christians.

    The Chi-Rho symbol

Other secret signs included the picture of a fish (Greek: 'Ichthus'). Its hidden meaning? **I**esous **Christos**, **Th**eoun **U**ios (or Yios) **S**oter, meaning 'Jesus Christ, Son of God, Saviour'.

After printing with moveable type was invented (in 1436, in Germany), Christian scholars throughout Europe hurried to publish Bibles, service-books, and their own writings. To save time – and paper – they began to use 'Xmas' instead of 'Christmas'. Since then, the word has spread round the world. But early printers' shorthand 'Xtian' = 'Christian' has not been so widely copied.

Xmas = Xtra-special?

Because Christmas was such a special, holy day, past people believed that anyone born then would also be special.

Birthday on Christmas Day? Then these old superstitions – true or false – might interest, or alarm, you!

- You'll never see – or be frightened by – a ghost.

- You'll never be drowned or hanged.

- You'll always be lucky.

- BUT, at least in Poland, there's a danger that you might turn into a werewolf!

- According to a poem written around AD 1525: if Christmas is a Sunday, the baby will be a great lord; a Monday, he will be strong and keen; a Tuesday, he will be greedy; a Wednesday, brave and cheery; a Thursday, always happy; a Friday, long-lived and loving. But if Christmas falls on a Saturday, in six months he will die!

Birthday names

Parents also gave children names to help them remember the special day when they were born – or else simply in honour of Jesus's birthday. Most of these names are based on the Latin words 'dies natalis' which mean 'day of birth'. They include Nathalie (French), Noel, Noelle (English, French), Natividad or Nati (Spanish), Natalia (Greek, Russian) and Natasha (Russian).

Famous Xmas names

Noelle, Countess Rothes (1884–1956) Survivor of the Titanic shipwreck. She bravely helped others while waiting to be rescued.

Noel Coward (1899–1973) Actor, singer, dramatist, songwriter. Scandalous but witty and stylish. Wrote the famous number: 'Mad Dogs and Englishmen Go Out in the Midday Sun'.

Natalia Pognina (born 1985) World-class chess player; one of the very few women ever to win the rank of Grandmaster.

Father Christmas?

Other Xmas names include 'Christmas' itself as a surname. According to the 1990 United States government Census, it ranked 4,757 out of 88,799 different family names.

The same name also appears in Russian: 'Rozhdestvo' (Christmas) becomes Rozhdestvensky (for men) and Rozhdestvenskaia (for women).

In 2005, genetics scientists at Oxford University announced a plan to study men in England called 'Christmas'. They hoped to discover whether – or not – they are all descended from a single male ancestor.

Wait! Something else is puzzling me! At the start of this chapter we mentioned the date 'around AD 1770'. But how do we know which year it is? Who fixed year one, and started counting? And what does 'AD' mean?

DENNIS SOLVES DATING DILEMMA

READERS! DENNIS HAS DONE IT! TODAY WE CAN ANNOUNCE A WORLD-CHANGING BREAKTHROUGH BY MATHEMATICAL MONK DIONYSIUS EXIGUUS (DENNIS THE VERY SMALL). SEVEN YEARS AGO, LEADERS OF THE CHRISTIANS FACED A CHURCH CALENDAR CRISIS! THEY NEEDED NEW LISTS OF YEARS TO HELP THEM WORK OUT WHEN EASTER SHOULD BE CELEBRATED.[1]

EXISTING LISTS OF YEARS WERE BASED ON THE REIGNS OF ROMAN EMPERORS. BUT DENNIS DISAPPROVED – MANY OF THOSE EMPERORS HAD PERSECUTED CHRISTIANS! SO HE DECIDED TO DRAW UP LISTS STARTING WITH A NEW FIXED POINT IN THE PAST. HE CHOSE THE TIME THAT JESUS CHRIST WAS CONCEIVED. A NEAT IDEA. WELL DONE, DENNIS!

DATELINE: AD 532

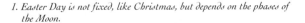

1. *Easter Day is not fixed, like Christmas, but depends on the phases of the Moon.*

The rest, as they say, is history. For a while, Dennis's lists of years were only used for calculating the date of Easter. But news of them spread, and, in AD 731, one of the world's most respected scholars, an English monk called Bede, wrote 'A History of the English People'. In it, he copied Dennis by counting years from the date that Jesus appeared on Earth. Other monks used any empty space on each page of their copies of Dennis's lists to note important events, year by year. A whole new way of recording time had been invented!

Today, most people still use this dating system. They count forward to the present moment from the year AD 1, and backwards into the distant past from 1 BC, which means 'Before Christ'. There is no year 0 (zero) in between them. 'AD' stands for 'Anno Domini': Latin for 'in the year of Our Lord' (Jesus) – that is, the year since Jesus was born.

Timed out!

The AD-BC way of counting years made history-writing easier. But the years in Dennis's list were not based on accurate observations of the Sun. Nor were the Church calendars that followed his example, used almost everywhere in Europe. After several centuries, these were seriously out-of-step with reality. By AD 1550, the Church year was around 11 days longer than a year in real time.[1] Something had to be done!

1. Today, astronomers say that an average year is 365.2425 days long.

Go, Gregory, go!

In 1582, Pope Gregory XIII volunteered for the challenge. As leader of the largest (Roman Catholic) Church in Europe, only he had the power. He decided to make the Church calendar catch up with the Sun – by getting rid of its extra 11 days. Most people were horrified. They felt that the Pope had robbed them, and their lives would now be shorter. They demanded, 'Give us our days back!'

A few Catholic kings agreed to enforce the New Style, or 'Gregorian', calendar in their lands. But Protestants refused to follow it. Gregory's reforms took almost 200 years to be accepted throughout Europe. For all that time, Christmas was celebrated on different days, Old Style or New Style, in different kingdoms. A traveller going from one kingdom to another could enjoy Christmas twice!

England did not change its calendar until 1752, when an Act of Parliament ordered that Old 2nd September must be followed by New 13th September. Bulgaria, the last country to change, used the Old Style calendar until – astonishingly – 1968.

On the twelfth day of Christmas
My true love gave to me
Twelve lords a leaping
Eleven ladies dancing
Ten pipers piping
Eight maids a milking
Seven swans a swimming
Five golden rings
Four colley[1] birds
Three French hens
Two turtle doves[2]
And a partridge in a pear tree![3]

The first-known English version of these words dates from around AD 1250, but they were probably composed even earlier, in France. Originally, the song was a memory game. Players took turns to sing a verse. If they got the words wrong, they had to pay a forfeit.

In 2009, it was calculated that the gifts listed above would cost almost USD $90,000.

1. blackbirds
2. traditional signs of true love
3. EITHER the devil's bird plus a magic fertility symbol OR, more likely, mis-remembered French words that originally meant something like 'part of a juniper tree'.

Chapter Four

The Twelve Days of Christmas

...and before

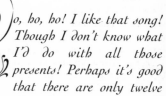

Ho, ho, ho! I like that song! Though I don't know what I'd do with all those presents! Perhaps it's good that there are only twelve days of Christmas. I wonder who invented them, and why? What's the reason for the season?

Tours, France
AD 567

Greetings, brother monks!

You wouldn't believe how busy I've been, here at this Church Council. So many bishops, from all over Western Europe! So many meetings! So much politics! But we've made good progress, and now I can share some exciting news with you. The Council declares that we can celebrate Christmas for 12 whole days (and nights)! The Twelve Days of Christmas will start after dark on 25 December and end on 6th January.

Old pagan festivals, such as Yule, lasted for a week or more, so people expect a long break at midwinter. And our new Twelve Days will link Christmas Day with another special date: the 6th January, when Eastern Christians celebrate Jesus's baptism. That should end the holiday season nicely!

I start my journey home to our monastery tomorrow, but it may be weeks before I see you. My horse is so slow, and the roads are so muddy!

Blessings to you

Willibald (Abbot)

Stop! Wait a minute! Aren't we forgetting something? What about ADVENT, just BEFORE Christmas? That's a special time, too!

Waiting for God

As soon as the early Church had fixed the date of Christmas Day, it also began to teach its followers that they should make preparations for it. For four weeks, starting on the first Sunday after 30 November, they should fast (go without meat) and say extra prayers asking God to forgive their sins. In Poland, people also gave thanks to Mary, for being Jesus's mother.

Early Christians called this time of waiting and praying 'Advent' (from Latin 'adventus' = arriving). It was gloomy and sorrowful, especially on Thursdays, when "dreadful devils" escaped from Hell to tempt Christian men and women. On the same days – can this be coincidence? – gangs of teenagers roamed the streets, 'bouncing and beating on every door'. The only way to get rid of them was to offer dried fruit – a luxury in midwinter – or money.

For Christian believers, Advent was also a time of hope and longing. This sometimes included most the un-Christian practice of fortune-telling. Northern farmers forecast the weather, by quoting dismal proverbs such as 'Barbara brings bridges'.[1]

Further south, around the shores of the Mediterranean Sea, sailors continued to believe in an Ancient Greek forecast. For seven days before and seven days after the Winter Solstice, there would be fine, calm, weather. Why? Because the Halcyon, a mythical bird, builds its nest then, on the sea. The water stays peaceful until the bird's eggs have hatched, 14 days later.

Much more cheerfully, young, unmarried girls tried to find out about their future husbands during Advent. There were at least three ways to do this:

1. St Barbara's Day is 4 December. The 'bridges' were ice; frozen lakes and rivers.

MARRIAGE MAGIC – TRY THESE SPELLS!

- Take as many onions as you have boyfriends. Mark each with a sign; one for each of your sweethearts. Put the onions in a warm place and wait patiently. The first to sprout green shoots will reveal your future husband.

- Go to the woodstack in the back yard after dark, and pull out a small stick. If it's straight, your future husband will be good and kind; if it's twisted or knotted – oh, bad luck! – he'll be mean and miserable.

- Go to the pigstye late one night. Call to the pigs and wait for them to answer. If a big pig grunts first, you'll marry an old man; if it's a small pig, you'll wed a young one!

Even for Christians, Advent was not all gloom and self-denial. Here are some examples of Advent cheer:

From the end of November, 'Christkindlesmärkte' (Christmas Markets) were held in north and central Europe. First recorded in the German city of Nuremberg in 1638, these after-dark gatherings were a mixture of open-air shopping and cheerful neighbourhood parties. In candle-lit, decorated streets, stalls sold toys, gifts and

Christmas ornaments. Shoppers strolled while choirs sang Christmas carols. The Nuremberg market was opened by the 'Christ-Child' – not Jesus, but a pretty young girl.

On 5 December, parents in Germany and the Netherlands promised children that St Nicholas would bring them presents – or punishments – at bedtime! (You can read more about this on page 127.) At the same time, everyone nibbled gingerbread, to honour him.

St Nicholas never visited Britain (in real life, or in legends), but English schoolboys celebrated his day (6 December) by choosing a Boy Bishop. They dressed him in rich robes or, sometimes, as a woman. He gave orders, demanded respect, led singing, dancing and begging in the streets, and even preached sermons. Religious reformers disapproved of such "superstitious and childysshe" activities. But Boy Bishops were useful. They let weak people – women, children, the poor – challenge the rich and powerful without causing too much trouble.

Countdown to Christmas

Advent calendars were invented in Germany. The oldest-known, cut and painted by hand, was made in 1851. Before this, pious familes hung up little holy pictures, day by day, or marked time from 1st until 24 December by chalking a line on the wall. By around 1903, cheap colour printing made it possible to mass-produce Advent calendars, and they became very popular. Opening little windows to reveal hidden pictures fascinated children and adults.

Halfway through Advent (and, in the Old Style calendar, on the shortest day of the year), take time off from prayer and fasting to join in this joyful festival.

You'll have to go to Sweden to see it at it's best.
Here! Hop on my sleigh!

Light in darkness

Lucia! The name means 'light', and indeed the sunlight grows stronger after her festival. St Lucy or Lucia (died around AD 304), was a beautiful, holy maiden. Rather than marry, she tore out her eyes. Miraculously, they were returned – but, soon after, she was killed for being a Christian. Lucy was honoured in Italy, her homeland, and in northern Europe, on 13 December. There, her festival fell at the same time as an old, pre-Christian celebration. Called Lussi Night, it was a time when an evil witch flew through the air, bringing trolls and ghosts to haunt the darkness. Families sat up until daybreak to make sure that their homes stayed safe.

In Scandinavia (and places where Scandinavians have settled), a young girl is still chosen as Lucia for the day. Dressed in white, with a crown of lighted candles, she leads a procession of singers. Girls who follow her wear silver head-dresses and carry yellow cakes, ginger cookies and candles; boys hold lanterns and have hats decorated with stars.

But times have changed. Instead of keeping watch for Lussi ghosts, Swedish people now hold all-night parties. And, in 2008, equal-opportunity-aware Swedish students elected a boy to be their school's 'Lucia', but he was barred from the role.

Let me tell you about more candles – this time, wrapped in red ribbon. These were first handed out to Czech children in Advent 1747, to remind them that Jesus is 'the Light of the World'. Since around 1960, the candle has been stuck into oranges and decorated with dried fruit. Today this festive handful[1] is called a Christingle (Christ Kindl = Little Christ-Child).

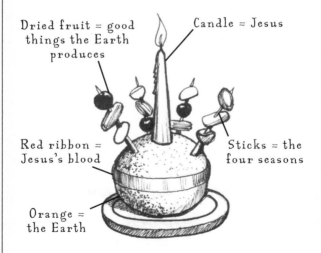

Dried fruit = good things the Earth produces

Candle = Jesus

Red ribbon = Jesus's blood

Sticks = the four seasons

Orange = the Earth

---

1. *A handful indeed; it's slippery, prickly, and drips hot wax and orange juice!*

Let's go mumping!

St Thomas's Day, 21 December, was the third time in Advent when rich families in England were expected to give generously to the poor. Children smeared their faces with soot and went 'A-Thomasing' or 'A-Mumping', to beg for money. From St Thomas's Day to Twelfth Night, troops of guisers or mummers – all men – also demanded payment. Dressed in masks with animal heads, or hidden under tattered, ragged costumes, they danced and sang, performed an ancient play – and probably used their disguises as cover while committing serious crimes. In the 16th century, King Henry VIII made wearing masks a crime, punishable by three months in prison.

In Germany it was said that 'a good meal on St Thomas's Day means you will eat well throughout the year'. A fat pig – your own or a stolen one – was the ideal dinner. And the last student to get out of bed that day was called a 'Lazy Thomas Donkey'.

Beware the Christmas Cat...

No, not a cuddly children's toy or even a real-life kitten, the Christmas Cat was a very nasty monster! In northern Europe it was most unlucky to leave work – such as spinning thread or sewing clothes – unfinished at Christmas. In Iceland, farmers traditionally gave new garments to their workers then, and parents gave clothes to their children. If they had not got these ready by 23 December, the Christmas Cat – or a frightful goblin called Torlak – would come to get them!

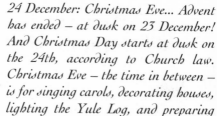

24 December: Christmas Eve... Advent has ended – at dusk on 23 December! And Christmas Day starts at dusk on the 24th, according to Church law. Christmas Eve – the time in between – is for singing carols, decorating houses, lighting the Yule Log, and preparing very special meals for friends and relatives. You can read about all these in Chapters 1, 5, 6 and 7.

In Poland on Christmas Eve, friends kissed and exchanged oplatek (wafer-biscuits stamped with religious pictures); in Finland, the Christmas Peace was declared:

"Tomorrow, God willing, is the most gracious feast of the birth of our Lord and Saviour, and therefore a general Christmas peace is hereby declared, and all persons are directed to observe this holiday with due reverence and otherwise quietly and peacefully to conduct themselves...."

Everywhere, the evening of 24 December was the time to go to Church. For many believers, it was the holiest, most magical night of the year. Around midnight, farm animals were said to kneel, honouring the hour when Jesus was born. If you were very fortunate (and quiet) you might hear them talking. Out in the fields, you might also see sheep bowing three times towards Bethlehem.

Much, much more noisily, Christmas Eve was also a time for bell-ringing. For example, in Dewesbury, Yorkshire, 'Black Tom of Soothill' (a great bell over 700 years old) was – and still is – rung once for each year since Jesus was born, with the peal ending at midnight. After that, the bell is rung just one more time, to tell the Devil of Jesus's birth, and to protect the town. In southern and eastern Europe, villagers fired guns or set off fireworks instead, to scare evil spirits away.

Christmas Eve is one of my busiest times, of course! So, on 25 December, I'm utterly exhausted. I usually rest, but for everyone else it's the start of Twelve (mostly) fun-filled Days! Here's my Christmas Checklist, to guide you!

25 December: Christmas Day

• *Ring bells (again)*

• *Go to church (again)*

• *Open presents (perhaps – see page 129)*

• *Put on your best clothes.*

• *Go to visit your family.*

(cont. overleaf)

When Christmas was banned

In 1644, Puritans (people with strong Protestant beliefs) ruled England, Wales, Scotland and Ireland. They thought that old Christmas traditions – from mince pies to Midnight Mass – were wrong, and forbade them. For 16 years, until the Puritan government was replaced by Catholic King Charles II in 1660, Christmas celebrations were forbidden. And Christmas stayed unpopular in Scotland for centuries.

DECEMBER 25

- *Give food to the poor, and/or invite your neighbours to dinner. If you're Polish or Czech, you'll lay an extra place, just in case baby Jesus calls at your home.*

- *If you're royal or noble, appoint a 'Lord of Misrule' to organise music, dancing, party-games, and masques (plays with music and dancing) to entertain your house-guests until Twelfth Night (6 January). Although only a servant, the temporary 'Lord' will be free to give orders, play tricks, tell jokes and tease – or annoy! – everyone at your party, no matter how important. Ho, ho, ho!*

- *Listen to the Waits – night-watchmen – and pay them. They visit rich houses to sing carols for money. Gangs of poor, hungry children do the same. Have pity on them! Troops of Sword-Dancers, Goose-Dancers (men dressed as girls, and vice-versa) and Mummers (see page 79) might also visit you at any time during the Twelve Days of Christmas.*

- *If you're a farmer, the weather is a constant worry: If Christmas Day is a Sunday, it will be fine all year. If a Monday, expect extreme weather. If a Tuesday, disastrous! If a Wednesday, cold winter, hot summer. If a Thursday, wild spring, but a fruitful summer. If a Friday, a dry summer, and sheep and bees will die. If a Saturday, snowy winter, 'evil' summer!*

84

- *Staying in south-west England? Then go see the Glastonbury Thorn. It's said to bloom every Christmas – flowery twigs are sent to the king or queen. Legends tell how the first thorn came from Joseph of Arimathea, the man who gave up his own tomb so that Jesus's body could be buried. He visited Glastonbury, stuck his walking stick into the ground – and it blossomed!*

- *Sing, sing, sing! In Wales, get up at 3am to to chant carols, and don't stop until daybreak. Why? The noise drives evil spirits from farms.*

- *Check your sums! Finalise your accounts! Don't neglect your business! Christmas is a Quarter Day – one of the four days each year when rents are paid and bills have to be settled. Lawyers, farm managers, rent-collectors and bailiffs will have lots to do this morning.*

- *In Scotland, eat 'care-cakes' in bed (they're baked in honour of the Virgin Mary). But don't go back to sleep – remember, you have to work as usual. In many parts of Europe, Christmas was a working day for ordinary people. The Scots did not make Christmas a public holiday until 1958.*

- *Late at night, if you're not too tired, try a little fortune-telling! Gaze at the sky! A waxing (increasing) moon promises a good year, a waning (decreasing) moon a bad one. And shooting stars mean lots of babies...*

26 December –
1st Day of Christmas

- *Feast of St Stephen – the first Christian martyr. He was stoned to death around AD 35 for claiming that Jesus was the Messiah. He is the patron saint of builders – and headaches!*

- *Are you in Ireland? Then catch a wren and kill it, or carry it from house to house in a cage of holly branches while begging for money. Why mistreat a poor little bird? Traditionally, a wren betrayed St Stephen to his killers. But remember: "Those who kill a robin or wren, Will never prosper, boy or man." (Traditional rhyme, Cornwall)*

- *Are you rich? And English, Welsh or Irish? Is the date sometime between AD 1600 and 2005? Then get on your horse, and go hunting! Boxing Day is a traditional time to chase and kill a fox. Some claim it's great sport; others say it's 'the unspeakable chasing the uneatable'.*

- *Another horsy tradition – running races on Boxing Day – is even older. It may date back to Viking times (around AD 800–1100).*

- *"Good King Wenceslas looked out, On the Feast of Stephen..." The trouble is, he probably didn't. Duke Vaclav (= Wenceslas) of Bohemia died in AD 935; he was murdered by pagans. Vaclav was famous for Christian good deeds, but the words of this well-known carol, written in 1853, tell an invented story.*

- St Stephen's Day was, however, a traditional time for giving to the poor. In England and Wales, it's Boxing Day! Nothing to do with prize-fighting, but the time to hand out 'Christmas Boxes': gifts to people who have worked for you during the past year.

- Some Boxing Day presents are food and drink but more often they are money. Occasionally – in mean households – servants are simply given cloth, so they can sew their own new uniforms.

Well, that may be ONE reason for the name 'Boxing Day'! Here is another. Both may be right – or neither!

- In the past, each church had a Poor-Box: a big wooden chest where people could leave gifts for charity. Once a year, around Midwinter, this chest was opened, and its contents were shared among the poor.

JANUARY   FEBRUARY

87

27 December –
2nd Day of Christmas

- Feast of St John, one of Jesus's disciples (first followers). He's believed to protect against poison.

- In Germany, share a drink with friends from a loving-cup, a big cup that is filled and passed around at a feast. Its contents will be safe to consume – St John will protect you!

- And look out for 'Star-Singers'; from today until 6 January. In German-speaking lands, they might visit your home dressed as the Wise Men plus their guiding star. Once they've sung, they will scribble the date of their visit above your front door. Don't wash the writing away – it brings good luck!

28 December –
3rd Day of Christmas

- Holy Innocents Day. This mourns the babies at Bethlehem who were killed on King Herod's orders (see page 40).

- Take care – traditionally, it's a very unlucky day! Make sure you don't:
        Put on new clothes
        Cut your nails
        Begin a new project

NOVEMBER					DECEMBER				
M	3	10	17	24	M	1	8	15	22	29
T	4	11	18	25	T	2	9	16	23	30
W	5	12	19	26	W	3	10	17	24	31
T	6	13	20	27	T	4	11	18	25	
F	7	14	21	28	F	5	12	19	26	
S	1	8	15	22	29	S	6	13	20	27	
S	2	9	16	23	30	S	7	14	21	28	

- *Living in Spain – or another Spanish-speaking country? Then keep your wits about you! Today's the day when your friends will try to make you believe the most absurd stories, or play practical jokes on you. If you fall for their tricks, they'll call you 'inocente!', which means 'fool' as well as 'young child'.*

29 December –
4th Day of Christmas

- *Norwegian? Keep on lighting those candles – one for every day from Christmas Eve to New Year! And check the sheaf of wheat that you've left outside to feed the birds in the Christmas cold – and the rice porridge that you leave for the Nisse (elves) who guard your farm animals.*

- *Anywhere: look out for flies! It's very unlucky if one comes into your house between Christmas and New Year.*

30 December –
5th Day of Christmas

- *Cut wood today – it will never rot. But don't plough or spin wool.*

- *Clean and tidy your house (and your office), ready for New Year.*

31 December –
6th Day of Christmas: New Year's Eve

So much to do today,
especially if you're Scottish!

VOLUNTEERS WANTED
FOR ONE NIGHT ONLY
☞ YOUR NEIGHBOURS NEED YOU ☜

* Take part in tradition *
* Bring good luck *

Are you a Man with a Scottish accent?
Tall, dark and handsome?
Got a lump of coal and a glass in your hand?
(Kilt preferred, but not essential)

LIGHT DUTIES	OPTIONAL EXTRAS
Just knock on the front door at midnight and enter. You do not have to sing 'Auld Lang Syne'.	Open doors or windows in the home to let the old year out and the new year in.

NO PAY, BUT WARM WELCOME
GUARANTEED

PLUS WEE DRAM WITH SHORTBREAD OR BLACK BUN[1]

1. See page 115.

You may find, however, that some of your neighbours are otherwise occupied:

"On New Year's Eve, they surrounded each other's houses carrying dried cow-hides and beating them with sticks, thrashing the walls with clubs, all the time crying, shouting and repeating rhymes... as a charm against fairies, demons and spirits..."

Supersitions of the [Scottish]
Highlanders, 1878

Or you could join Scottish children, begging for oat-cakes:

Au gui l'an neuf![1]

1. *'Good health to the New Year!' (French). Say this quickly and it sounds – a bit – like 'Hogmany', a Scottish name for New Year's Eve. Well, no-one has come up with a better suggestion for the origin of the name so far.*

Footprints from the future?

If you're feeling brave, you might like to try this ancient New Year's Eve custom.

- Late at night, spread the ashes smoothly on the hearth.

- By morning, you should find a footprint in them.

- If it points towards the door, a family member will die. If it points inwards, there will be a new baby!

Kisses and wishes

But this might be more fun:

"As soon as ever the clock struck one, I kissed my wife... Wishing her a Merry New Year. I believe I was the first proper wisher of it this year..."

Samuel Pepys, Diary, 31 January 1664

And remember: Keep your table full of food all night long, to make sure you have enough to eat in the coming year. BUT, if you want to please the priests, ignore tradition and don't wear a mask, buy lucky charms, dance wildly through the streets, or get drunk.

"Say no ill of the year, till it be past."

Traditional proverb

Ring Out Wild Bells

Ring out wild bells, to the wild sky,
The flying cloud, the frosty night:
The year is dying in the night,
Ring out wild bells, and let him die.

Ring out the old, ring in the new,
Ring, happy bells, across the snow
The year is going, let him go;
Ring out the false, ring in the true...

Alfred, Lord Tennyson (1809–1892)

1 January – 7th Day of Christmas:
New Year's Day

I wish, I wish...

In many parts of Europe, New Year, not Christmas, was the time for gift-giving (you can read more about this on page 129). It was also a time for offering bribes to kings and law-court judges in England, and for making New Year's resolutions – a habit that continues today. In 2010, the United States Government website listed the following top ten – no, eleven – wishes:

• Drink less alcohol
• Get a better education
• Get a better job
• Get fit
• Lose weight
• Manage debt
• Stop smoking
• Reduce stress
• Save money
• Take a trip
• Volunteer to help others

What a worry!

After Christmas fun and games, New Year's day a was a fresh – and uncertain – beginning. Who could tell what the future held in store? Anxious familes 'dipped' into the Bible (opened pages at random, read the words as prophecies) or did their best to take control of the unknown...

Be careful what you do today – it can set the pattern for the whole of the coming year:

- To stay active: get up early. **YAWN!**
- To have a job: spend a few minutes doing your usual daily work, even though it's a holiday. **GROAN!**
- To have food: bring fresh bread into the house. **YUM!**
- To have clothes; wear something new today. **PRETTY!**
- To have money: pay your debts. And pop a few coins into all family members' pockets. **THANKS!**
- To be lucky: don't sweep dust or ashes ouside, and don't throw out slops or dirty water. **YUCK!**
- Above all, **DON'T WASH** clothes, dishes or maybe even yourself – you'll wash a family member away, forever!

In the Scottish Highlands, one thing that always had to be brought in fresh and first thing on New Year's Day was 'the Cream of the Well': icy-cold spring water. An alternative was water from a fast-running burn (stream) – traditionally, the boundary between the dead and the living. This was solemnly sprinkled all round the house – including the beds, with people still sleeping in them. At the same time, each home was filled with smoke from smouldering juniper bushes.

These good-luck ceremonies were sure to keep witches away, but did NOT improve Hogmanay hangovers! Sometimes, they were even more startling:

"In Glenlyon, Scotland, the landlady takes care to rise early on the morning of New Year's Day. She ties together some straw in the form of a brush, and sprinkles urine with it upon the whole family as they are getting out of bed."

J. Ramsay, *Scotland in the 18th Century*, Vol 2, 1888

2 January –
8th Day of Christmas

After Hogmany celebrations, and New Year rituals
and worries – ZZZZZZZZZZZZZ!

3 January –
9th Day of Christmas

No special celebrations, but you could shine a light
in honour of St Genevieve (died AD 512), whose
feast day this is. She bravely kept on praying in the
dark while the devil blew out her candle. An angel lit
it for her again!

Or, perhaps like King Arthur in this medieval poem,
you'll still be feasting:

> The king held his Christmas court at Camelot...
> Many fine lords...
> Shared his joy, free of care, and his cheerful games...
> They all relished revelling for fifteen days,
> With all the food and fun that anyone could wish for:
> So much joyful noise, such jolly laughter
> Each daytime...
> ...each night, dancing...

(Anon, 'Sir Gawain and the Green Knight',
14th century)

WEEK 52
363-6

4 January –
10th Day of Christmas

If you're a farmer or a sailor, and you're still worrying about future weather, perhaps this traditional lore will help you. Look at the weather today. What's it like? Make a note, because it will be the same in November.

5 January – 11th Day of Christmas:
Twelfth-Day Eve

Almost the end of Christmas now. But wait! WHAT ABOUT THE WASSAILERS?

> *Here we come a-wassailing,*
> *Among the leaves so green,*
> *Here we come a wandering,*
> *So fair to be seen.*

> *Love and joy come to you*
> *And to you your wassail too,*
> *And God bless you*
> *And send you a Happy New Year*
> *And God send you a Happy New Year.*

(Words traditional English, probably 17th century)

The eve of Epiphany

"...On the eve of Epiphany [ie 5 January], the farmer, attended by his workman, with a large pitcher of cyder, goes into the orchard, and there, encircling one of the best bearing trees, they drink the following toast several times:

Here's to thee, old apple tree,
Whence thou may't bud
And whence thou may'st blo!
And whence thou may bear apples enow!
Hats full! Caps full!
And my pockets full too! Huzza!"

(Report in The Gentleman's Magazine, 1791)

In other orchards, cider was poured onto the apple trees, or toasted bread soaked in cider was placed among their branches.

You may think it's strange to offer drink to apple trees, but that's what wassailing is all about. With a name taken from two Old Norse words ('ves heill' = good health!) wassailing is a very ancient West-of-England tradition. It aims to protect and make plentiful all the orchards that grow there. Here's an alternative way of wassailing:

- Build 12 fires in a circle in a farmer's wheat-field.
- Light a thirteenth fire in the centre of the circle, taller than the rest.
- Stand round the circle, and drink to the health of the farmer – and the field – while the fires burn.
- Find a cow with a crooked horn. Stick a cake on her horn, and splash her face with cider.
- The cow will shake its head, and the cake will fall off. Watch where it lands. In front of the cow – there will be a good harvest. Behind the cow – crops will fail.

Wassailers also filled a huge, decorated bowl with cider, and walked – or stumbled – around their home villages, going from door to door to drink the health of each household. Friendly householders invited wassailers inside for 'lambs' wool' (hot spiced ale with fluffly baked apple pulp).

6 January –
12th Day of Christmas

- Feast of the Epiphany (a word of Greek origin, meaning 'God appearing on Earth') and of Jesus's baptism as a young man. Christians in the East celebrate these events today as their main midwinter festival, rather than Christ's birthday. Christians in western Europe remember the Wise Men who brought gifts to baby Jesus (see page 40).

- In Britain? Your Christmas decorations must be removed by this morning. Then they must be burnt, or fed to the cattle, or buried. No-one can agree — except that doing the wrong thing brings terrible bad luck. In Germany and Austria, decorations can remain in place until Candlemas (2 February).

- Tonight, Twelfth Night, is the traditional time for going to the theatre (or even, if you are William Shakespeare, writing a special play for the occasion, called 'Twelfth Night'). Living in colonial America? Then, like Cinderella, you may go to the Twelfth Night ball.

- Fancy a flutter? Rich enough to risk absolutely everything? Then hurry to the palace. This is the time of year that the King of England and his courtiers begin to gamble with cards and dice.

- *Out in the country? Tough and strong? Then join in the Haxey Hood Game. It commemorates a lovely Lady of the Manor, whose hood blew off in the winter wind. Now, 700 years later, teams of 'Boggins' (men from rival villages) still fight to get hold of a 'hood' (rope wrapped in leather) and carry it back to their local public house. This can take several hours.*

After all this fun, there's just time for another, final, feast, in honour of the Wise Men. Then for everyone, the holiday's over and it's back to work again.

Ever wondered why the first working day after 6 January was called 'Plough Monday'?

It's the day when farm-hands start work in the fields. Among women, the same day was known as 'Rock (Wool-Spinning) Monday'.

> *"At Christmas be merye,*
> *and thankful withall*
> *And feast thy poore neighbours*
> *ye gret with ye small..."*

Poet Thomas Tusser, England, c 1550

An unhappily quiet Christmas:

"...there were none of the [usual] disguisings[1], harp-playing, lute music, singing, or lewd sports[2]; just backgammon, chess and cards. Those were the only games that she [a noble lady] gave her servants and tenants permission to play..."

Letter from Margaret Paston,
England, 1485

1. *Mummers' plays and other rough, noisy dramas.*
2. *Rowdy party games*

Chapter Five

Eat, drink and be merry

Ho, ho, ho! Welcome, one and all! Welcome to my... well, what shall I call it: Christmas Dinner? Julbord? Le Reveillon? Drei Konigs Tag? These festive feasts have so many different names – one for each country. And they're held on different days, as well: Christmas Eve, Christmas Day, New Year's Eve or Twelfth Night. Not that I'm complaining! If I'm lucky – and well organised – I can enjoy at least FOUR fantastic meals, plus plenty of tasty snacks, during the Christmas season. And, once the meals are over, I can join in the carol-singing, dancing and party-games as well!

*So hurry over here! Hop aboard my
sleigh! Come with me on a gastronomic
tour of past Christmas specialities! There
are so many dishes to choose from, we
can't possibly see them all. But I'll try to
give you a just little taste (ha ha!).*

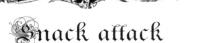

Snack attack

In Britain, you should eat a mince pie at a
different house on each of the Twelve Days of
Christmas. It's meant to bring good luck for
every month of the year.

Rich and sticky, traditional mince pies are made
of dried fruit, sugar, spices, salt, suet
(shredded beef fat) – and – yes, as the name tells
us – real meat, neatly minced into little tiny
pieces. Chopped liver, tongue or even fish can be
substituted.

Perhaps you'll have earned a year's good luck
after eating twelve fish-flavoured fruit pies!

Mince pies were banned in England in 1644
(see page 83). According to one British
national newspaper[1], eating them is still illegal
on Christmas Day.

1. *Sunday Mirror, 2008*

Too much!

Before you set off with Santa, just a few words of warning. Take care! Don't eat too much! Watch your waistline! Christmas was a very special time of year; a season when rules could be broken. For a short while, and only in traditional ways, rowdy, lazy, saucy – or extremely self-indulgent – behaviour was permitted. So when it came to mealtimes, greed was good! Instead of eating moderately, as the Church encouraged, everyone enjoyed as much as they could, at meals which lasted for hours. And, of course, Christmas was a time for sharing food with friends and neighbours, or giving it to the poor.

Even poor families treated themselves to richer, more luxurious food than they could usually afford. And nobles' feasts were spectacular. Like nine meals at one time, they were arranged in three 'services', each with three separate courses.

Over the Christmas season of 1289, one English noble and his 70 guests ate:

- 1 boar
- The best part of 3 bullocks
- 2 young calves
- 4 doves
- 4 pigs
- 60 chickens
- 8 partridges
- plus bread and cheese!

The grandest feasts ended with elaborate concoctions – in England, called 'sotelties' (subtleties, or clever displays). They were not designed to satisfy hunger – everyone had eaten more than enough, already – but to delight and amuse:

> "Four and twenty blackbirds,
> baked in a pie.
> When the pie was opened,
> the birds began to sing.
> Wasn't that a dainty dish
> to set before the king?!"

Free for all?

In 1314, a rich and powerful English bishop gave a Christmas feast for the workers on his manor. Each man received:

- 2 white-bread loaves
- a dish of beef and bacon with mustard
- chicken stew
- cheese

And as much ale as he could drink that day!

However, there's a sting in the tail of the bishop's generosity. The workers had to give him the hens – and the firewood to cook them, and maybe other food, too – as part of the rent they owed him for their cottages and farmland.

A Christmas riddle
When is a plum not a plum (1)?

When it's a sugarplum! That was the old name for shiny little balls of transparent boiled sugar – the ancestors of today's boiled sweeties. Why? Perhaps because they were sort-of plum-shaped, or perhaps because they were suspended by stalk-like threads to cool and solidify.

A famous Christmas entertainment, the ballet *The Nutcracker Suite* (first performed in Russia in 1892), tells the story of a child's magic journey to the Kingdom of Sweets, where she is greeted by the Sugarplum Fairy!

Hurry up! Hurry up! Climb aboard! All over Europe, the cooks are already busy! They've been cooking traditional dishes like this for hundreds of years.

See, we already have our *Festive Menu.*

It's Christmas Eve...

...so it must be fish! Remember, the Church teaches that the fasting time of Advent does not end until tomorrow. Meanwhile, tantalise your tastebuds with a choice from the following traditional dishes:

France – salt cod
Rich and creamy, soaked then slow-cooked
with olive oil and garlic.

❄ ❄ ❄ ❄ ❄ ❄

Italy – stewed eels
Tender and succulent, in a sauce of wine and herbs.
No tomatoes, of course! They've not yet reached
Europe from America.

❄ ❄ ❄ ❄ ❄ ❄

North Germany – pickled herring
Refreshingly sharp and tangy, served
with sour cream, dill and onions.

❄ ❄ ❄ ❄ ❄ ❄

South Germany and Austria – blue carp
No, not old and mouldy, but cooked in
boiling vinegar and pepper.

Don't fancy fish? Then dine in Russian style, on 'kutya' (barley porridge). Its plump grains are a sign of hope and new life, even in winter. Add honey for happiness and success, and poppy seeds, for peaceful rest. Now enjoy, enjoy, but save one last spoonful – and be sure to throw it at the ceiling! If the porridge sticks there, it's a sign that the bees will give you lots of honey next year!

Still feeling hungry? Then continue your meal like the southern French: indulge yourself in the "Thirteen Desserts". This buffet commemorates the twelve Holy Apostles – Jesus's friends and followers – plus baby Jesus.

Thirteen Desserts

- Almonds -
- Walnuts -
- Raisins -
- Figs or dates -
- Apples and Pears -
- Oranges or Tangerines -
- Grapes or Winter melon -
- Quince paste and Candied fruits -
- Pale nougat -
- Dark nougat -
- Cakes and cookies -
- Calisson (soft almond sweets) -
- Fougasse (sweet spiced bread) -

Everywhere, Christmas is a time for families – and for visiting. So here's a supernatural Scandinavian way of holding a family Christmas Eve party.

- Before you go to bed, make sure that you've left plenty of food and drink on the table.

- Spread a clean white cloth on one of the chairs.

- Next morning, inspect the cloth carefully. If you see black marks on it – oooh! That's seriously scary! Your ancestors have risen from their graves – scattering earth as they sat down – to enjoy your hospitality.

Christmas Morning… Rise and Shine! *We're off to England now – they know how to breakfast there! Feeling brave? Who'd like to try some Frumenty or Plum Pottage? They're both hot, thick, sweet and very, very stodgy.*

Frumenty
Plain and Simple, for Peasants[1]

- Whole wheat grains soaked in water overnight, then simmered in milk – by the fireside is best – for hours and hours and hours.

- If you can afford it, add cinnamon, a few raisins, or honey.

Plum Pottage
A Rich Mix, for the – erm – Rich

- Onions, pepper and spices, chopped carrots, minced beef or pork, suet, and dried fruit. Optional extra: breadcrumbs, to thicken.

- Boil them all together – overnight if you like – and it's ready!

1. The Scots eat something similar, called Sowans. That's the rough outer chaff of oat-grains, soaked and boiled until it's brown and sticky like treacle. Somehow, it tastes both sickly-sweet and sour. Do try some!

Did you know?

Plum pudding – later called Christmas pudding – was originally the same mixture as plum pottage, but tied inside a floured cloth, then boiled in a cauldron of water. Today, the meat and onions are left out, but some recipes still include suet and carrots.

Scots 'Black Bun' is much the same, but baked in a (very, very) solid pastry wrapper. And it's eaten at New Year, not Christmas.

Watch your step!

Either of these will 'stick to your ribs' and give you plenty of energy. But they'll almost certainly weigh you down as well. So perhaps it's wise to avoid them if you plan to take part in lots of Christmas-Day dancing!

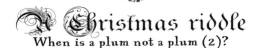

A Christmas riddle
When is a plum not a plum (2)?

When it's a dried grape of some kind: a currant, sultana or raisin. These were not brought in bulk to northern Europe before around AD 1500. Until then, the most common dried fruit cooked at midwinter was prunes (dried plums); the name survived for centuries in traditional Christmas dishes.

Ho, ho, ho! **Christmas Day Dinner!** *Let's stay in England for this, and enjoy a traditional roast. It will proably be served with bread, separate dishes of stewed leeks or greens – plus yet more dried fruit – and perhaps sharp and spicy sauces.*

• **Peacock and swan** ~ costly show-off foods, for nobles only.

- **Heron** ~ the smartest choice if you're a peasant, trying to impress, but first you have to catch one! Or else broil a bustard: a large bird rather like a monster chicken; by around 1840, hunted to extinction in England.

- **Goose** ~ a rich meat, best served German-style, stuffed with apples and prunes (yet again!)

In Victorian cities, poor families joined helpful neighbourhood 'Goose Club' savings schemes. If they paid in a few pence each week, they'd have enough to buy a goose for Christmas.

- **Wild boar** ~ the most traditional choice of all. The head is the best bit, believe me! It's either cooked, chopped, and compressed to make brawn, then served with vinegar and honey, or boiled and decorated with green herbs. The rest of the boar is eaten later, roasted.

Gobble, gobble

As (almost) everyone knows, turkeys do not come from Turkey. They were first domesticated in America, and unknown outside the Western Hemisphere until the 16th century. A Yorkshireman, William Strickland, is thought to have been the first to bring them to England. He purchased six from Native American traders, and landed them in Bristol in 1526.

At first, such exotic rarities could only be enjoyed by the super-rich – including King Henry VIII (ruled 1491-1547), Britain's first royal turkey eater.

By the 1700s, Norfolk farmers led flocks of turkeys on foot to London markets each winter. The turkeys were even supplied with specially-made leather boots for the journey. However, turkeys remained less popular than other Christmas meats until the late 19th century.

'What do you mean, it's only 80 miles? My feet are killing me!'

Even I'm feeling full of food, but there are still some Christmas treats waiting. Hop back on my sleigh and we'll whizz to Germany – and, perhaps, the USA – for cookies and, best of all, gingerbread! You know, that's changed a lot over the centuries…

Food and fairy-tales

The first gingerbread, made around AD 1200, was a mixture of breadcrumbs, honey and powdered ginger-root. This was cooked together, then poured into wooden moulds to cool and solidify. Before long, moulds were carved in the shape of animals or people. Gingerbread men had been invented!

No-one knows when the first gingerbread house was constructed. But a very sinister example features as a tempting trap for children in the story of Hansel and Gretel, published by German brothers Grimm in the early 19th century. Since then, building gingerbread houses has become a Christmas tradition, especially in the USA. Naturally,

the wicked witch in the Grimms' grim story did not provide instructions, but today's houses are made of crisp spicy biscuits, decorated with brightly-coloured icing sugar.

*Ho, ho, ho! Here I am! Back again! It's **New Year's Eve**, and so we're going to Scotland for a quick drink and a slice of Black Bun. Then, tomorrow morning, I must go to Italy and eat lentils. On New Year's Day, they're lucky! Because they look like coins, they'll make you rich for the coming year.*

'On the approach of twelve o'clock, a het [hot] pint was prepared – that is, a kettle or flagon full of warm, spiced and sweetened ale, with an infusion of spirits... each member of the family drank of this mixture: 'A good health and a happy New Year and many of them...'

19th century traveller's report on Scotland.

And to you all, dear readers!

Fit for three kings!

*Shhh! I think Santa's sleeping. He's exhausted by all this feasting and travelling. If he were awake, I'm sure he'd want to tell you about just one more Christmas tradition. It's the feast held on **Twelfth Night**, or **Epiphany** – the last day of the Christmas season in most parts of Europe.*

The main course can be any festive meat, but the dessert is very special. It's a cake looking like a crown – or decorated with crowns – in honour of the Wise Men in the gospel story. They are often (and mistakenly) called 'the Three Kings', and their cake contains a hidden secret. This can be a ring, a coin, or, more usually, a bean or little china figure representing baby Jesus. Whoever finds it in his slice of cake becomes king for the night – and leads the singing, dancing and party-games.

Now, Now the Mirth Comes

Now, now the mirth comes
With the cake full of plums
Where bean's the king of
the sport here...

Begin then to choose
This night as ye use
Who shall for the present delight here
Be a king by the lot
And who shall not...

English poet Robert Herrick (1591–1674)

" 'Twas the night before Christmas,
when all through the house
Not a creature was stirring,
not even a mouse.
The stockings were hung
by the chimney with care,
In hopes that St Nicholas
soon would be there..."

The famous first lines of a Christmas poem
by Clement Clarke Moore,
first published in 1823, in the USA.

"We three kings of Orient are
Bearing gifts, we traverse afar.
Field and fountain,
moor and mountain,
Following yonder star.
O Star of Wonder, Star of Night,
Star with Royal Beauty bright,
Westward leading, Still proceeding,
Guide us to Thy perfect Light..."

Christmas carol, written in the USA in 1857
by Rev J H Hopkins Jnr

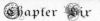

Chapter Six

Ho, ho, ho!

Gifts and gift-givers

Ho, ho, ho! I LOVE Christmas – it's a great time for giving! But, even though I'm so busy then, I still have time for thinking. I wonder: why do we exchange gifts at Christmas time? And why is it ME who has to bring them?

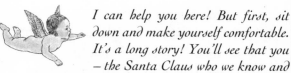

I can help you here! But first, sit down and make yourself comfortable. It's a long story! You'll see that you – the Santa Claus who we know and love today – has been created over 2000 years, by blending the following different traditions together. Let's begin at the beginning…

c 300 BC, Ancient Rome

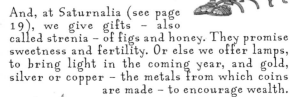

At midwinter, we cut twigs from the holy grove of the goddess Strenia, and hand them to our friends. They bring good fortune.

And, at Saturnalia (see page 19), we give gifts – also called strenia – of figs and honey. They promise sweetness and fertility. Or else we offer lamps, to bring light in the coming year, and gold, silver or copper – the metals from which coins are made – to encourage wealth.

Traces of Roman gift-giving customs survived in southern Europe until the 20th century. In France, for example, sweet gifts at New Year were called estrennes – the French way of saying 'strenia'.

c 100 BC,
Northern Europe

We honour – and fear – the Spirit of Midwinter. He's old and cold and a killer. We give gifts to HIM to try to keep him away.

c AD 350, Myra
(now in Turkey)

I'm Bishop Nicholas, and I died a few years ago. But to my surprise, I'm fast becoming famous – for miracles! Well, I did bring some young boys back to life. They'd been cut up and pickled, poor things; I found them in a barrel. I also saved a girl from being sold into slavery. How? Well, by posting gold coins down the chimney. Strange to say, the coins landed in her stocking, hung up in the fireplace to dry, and in her two sisters' stockings hanging close by. The money saved her family from starvation – and helped all three girls get married and live happily ever after.

c 1100 Bari, Italy

Nicholas again! Guess what? The Church has made me a saint! I protect children (of course!), and sailors, and thieves(!), and I'm the patron of Greece and Russia. In 1087, pirates from Sicily kidnapped my bones and brought them here, to a splendid new tomb. Crowds of pilgrims come to see it!

c 1200 – 1600, mainland Europe

On St Nicholas Eve,[1] that is, 5th December, we wait for the saint to visit us. We leave food for him before we go to bed, and put straw in our shoes to feed his horse. In memory of his miracles, he leaves us presents: toys or sweet treats if we've been good, or a stick (to punish us!) if we've been naughty.

Sometimes, St Nicholas is accompanied by scary friends and helpers, such as Knecht Ruprecht (Servant Rupert) in Germany, Sooty Peter (he climbs down the chimneys!) in the Netherlands, or, in Austria, Krampuses (see page 36) or the Klaubauf: a fearsome hairy monster with huge horns and a drooling red tongue.

Some of these 'helpers' are ancient nature-spirits that symbolise winter darkness and danger. By linking them to St Nicholas, the early Church 'tamed' them.

---

1. *The day before the Church Feast (holy-day) of St Nicholas, when he was remembered and honoured by special prayers.*

c 1400, England

In the British Isles, we prefer our ancient, pre-Christian, tradition of giving handsels (gifts) at midwinter, usually on New Year's Day.

Sometimes, we talk about 'Sire Christmas' (by around 1600, he'll also be known as 'Father Christmas'), but he does not bring presents, and is not especially fond of children. Instead, he's the spirit of jollity at midwinter festivals – and he's always dressed in bright green, like Christmas decorations.

c 1600 – 1800, Protestant countries in Europe (mostly in the north)

We Protestants disapprove of saint's days! So St Nicholas, please stay away! We like to think that baby Jesus, not you, brings gifts, to share at his birthday. So, in France look out for le Petit Jesus (Little Jesus) or le Pere Noel (Father Christmas); in Germany, you'll find the Weihnachtsmann (Holy Night Man) or the Christkindl (Christ Child; you've already met him on page 74). They'll bring you presents, just like St Nicholas used to, but at night, on Christmas Eve.

c 1600 – 1800
The Netherlands, Belgium and
northern Germany

Hey! Wait a minute! You can't get rid of me that quickly! As you can see, families here still look forward to the presents I bring – and still expect me to arrive, riding a beautiful white horse, on St Nicholas Eve. And bakers still cook wonderful gingerbread and biscuits, shaped like me and my helpers. What an honour!

c 1800, Russia

Something strange has happened to our cruel Spirit of Winter. He's mingling with Christian St Nicholas, and turning into a kindly gift-giver, called Ded Moroz (Grandfather Frost). He travels with a companion, a fairytale character called Snegurochka (Snow Maiden). She's very beautiful, but can't love or care – her heart is frozen. Stories tell how she meets a handsome young shepherd, and longs to fall in love with him. Her mother helps thaw her heart; she's happy for a brief moment – and then she dies.

c 1800, USA

Readers, guess what?! I've gone TRANSATLANTIC! Yes, Dutch and German settlers in the USA took me with them, from around 1650. At first, I stayed in their own little villages – or was even forgotten for a while – but, since around 1800, I've become popular again, nationwide. Scholars say that American colonists, fighting their hated British rulers from 1776–1783, chose me as their patron. They also began to honour their non-British ancestors, especially the Dutch, who founded the top trading city of New York.

In 1809, American author Washington Irving wrote a mock history book[1], making fun of this fashionable interest in St Nicholas – and inventing several new stories about me. In it, he changed me from a tall, thin, dignified religious leader in flowing robes and a mitre to a ridiculous comedy Dutchman, dressed in baggy breeches and a broad-brimmed hat.

Hmm – My horse has disappeared! An influential poem by Clement Clarke Moore, published in 1823, called 'A Visit from St Nicholas', says that I travel in a sleigh pulled by 'eight tiny reindeer'.

1. *"Diedrich Knickerbocker's History of New York from the Beginning of the World to the End of the Dutch Dynasty"*

This 'tradition' is very new: invented in an American picture-story book, 'The Children's Friend', in 1821. It's also very, very alarming to see that I've shrunk from a life-sized bishop into a tiny, chubby ELF...

It's 1863, and here's another change! German-born US artist Thomas Nast makes me older and very much fatter – but brings me back to life-size! He pictures me on the cover of 'Harpers Weekly' magazine, handing out gifts to wounded soldiers – and I'm dressed in the USA's proud Stars and Stripes flag. Next, in 1866, Nast turns me (well, all my clothes) bright red, fixing my public image for ever.

By now, my name has changed again, to Santa Claus. That's from German words: Sanct Herr Klaus = Holy Man [Ni]klaus, or perhaps from Dutch: 'Sinterklaes' (Sint [Ni]Claes, joined together).

In 1869 American poet George P. Webster gives me a new home, at the North Pole! There, I'm joined by tiny, green, toy-making elves – that idea was spread around by a US women's magazine, 'Godey's Lady's Book', in 1873. I'm also blended with, perhaps, just a touch of a Tomte.

c 1840s - 1870s
Scandinavia

Glaedelig Jul! I'm a Tomte, sometimes called a Nisse. Originally, I was an ancestor-spirit, watching over houses and farms. If I was well-treated, I helped farmers and housewives, but if I was ignored, then I could do a lot of harm. My bite is poisonous, and I can drive you mad, or make you dance with me until you drop dead from exhaustion. Traditionally, people give ME gifts at winter (usually porridge with butter). Any presents for children were brought by the Yule Goat.

But now! What a surprise! Look what's happened! I've been given a make-over! Swedish artist Jenny Nystrom has pictured me with a red coat, a long white beard and a friendly smile – and people say that I now bring Christmas presents. Possibly they're mixing me up with that new American Santa Claus – or blending us together.

Ho, ho, ho! Well! Who'd have thought it? So that's my history – but, even today, my story keeps on changing:

Santa Stories

1889 Santa Claus gets a wife! She first appears in print in a poem by American Katherine L Bates.

c 1890 First actor hired to impersonate Santa Claus in a department store, USA. And children start writing and posting letters to Santa Claus, creating a problem for many national Post Offices.

1897 In reply to a letter from an 8 year old girl, the New York Sun newspaper publishes an editorial, "Yes, Virginia, there is a Santa Claus". It praises children's willingness to believe in good things, and becomes world-famous.

c 1930 Russian Communist government moves Ded Moroz's visit from Christmas Eve to New Year's Day, and insist that he's dressed in blue. They want to break his links with Christian St Nicholas, and show that he's very different from America's Santa Claus.

1931 Coca-Cola corporation, USA, starts series of Christmas advertisements featuring a smiling, cola-drinking Santa Claus. But, contrary to later urban legends, they do NOT colour his costume to match the labels on their bottles. It's been red since the 1860s.

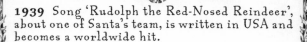

1939 Song 'Rudolph the Red-Nosed Reindeer', about one of Santa's team, is written in USA and becomes a worldwide hit.

1958 USA and Canada create NORAD (North American Air Defence Command) – a security system to keep watch for airborne invaders. At Christmas time, it also claims to track Santa's flight from the North Pole.

1982 Canadian Post Office creates a special zip code for letters to Santa: H0H 0H0.

1985 Santa Claus Village theme park opened at Rovaniemi, Finland. Visitors are invited to: '...meet Santa Claus and cross the Arctic Circle all year round'.

2007 It's claimed that 'the average person' in the UK spends £384 on Christmas gifts. Some of these, especially for children, are said to come from Santa.

2008 Canadian government minister declares that Santa is a Canadian citizen. Could this be linked to Canada's claims for a share of the North Pole region's rich natural resources?

And — MOST important — you're forgetting the other gift-givers who take over when my work is done: the Three Kings and Befana.

We Three Kings....

From around AD 500, Christian artists portrayed three richly-dressed kings offering gifts to new-born baby Jesus. At the same time, the Church in Western Europe celebrated their feast day on 6 January. But nowhere in the gospels mentions 'Three Kings' – or any three particular people visiting baby Jesus in Bethlehem. So who are they? Where does their story come from?

• Really royal?
As we saw on page 43, Jewish people living at the time of Jesus hoped for a Messiah to free them from Roman rule and set up a holy kingdom. Jewish prophecies said that kings would come to worship the Messiah, bringing royal gifts of gold and incense.

St Matthew's gospel describes 'Wise Men from the East' who brought gifts of gold, frankincense and myrrh (a bitter herb) to Jesus. Early Christians linked this story to the old Jewish prophecies, and thought that the wise men must also be kings.

• How many?

St Matthew's gospel does not say. At first, early Christians spoke of two visitors, or twelve, or four. But then they came to link the gifts and the givers. There were three gifts, so there must have been three royal visitors, they said. By around AD 500, they had given them royal names: Caspar, Melchior and Balthazar. By AD 700, each king also had a new identity: Caspar was young, and from the Mediterranean or maybe Europe. Melchior was old, and from Arabia or Asia. Balthazar was middle-aged and African.

• Wise Men or wizards?

At the time of Matthew's gospel, magi (astronomer-priests from Persia, now Iran) were famous for their knowledge of stars, planets and predictions. So, when Matthew wrote 'Wise Men', he was probably thinking of them. Confusingly, their name 'magi' also sounds like 'magic'. But the visitors to Bethlehem – if they ever reached there – were serious scholars.

• **Travelling on**
Some early Christian stories told how the Three Kings – or Wise Men – each lived to be over 100 years old, travelled to India, and died in Armenia. Adventurer Marco Polo claimed to have seen their tomb there, soon after AD 1300. But other tales told how the Three Kings' bodies were discovered by St Helena in AD 325. She took them to Constantinople (now Istanbul), and then a top bishop took them to Milan, in Italy. In 1163, Emperor Barbarossa from Germany attacked Milan, and carried off the Three Kings' bones – the city's greatest treasure.

Barbarossa took the bones to the cathedral in Cologne, Germany, where a huge, magnificent shrine of pure gold and glittering precious stones was made to contain them. It took 90 years to complete – and then a whole new cathedral was built, to shelter the shrine and visiting pilgrims. It became the largest medieval church in all Europe.

• More gift-giving

Even though the Three Kings' bones were imprisoned in gold, Christian legends told how they made a miraculous journey to Bethlehem, each Christmas time. Traditionally, children in Spain and the south of France learn that, if they're good, the Three Kings will call as they pass by, bringing them presents on 5th January.

Did you know that 6th January is also the feast of the Epiphany? That's a Greek word meaning 'appearance on Earth of a God'. And in Italy, children don't get presents from me, or from St Nicholas, or from the Three Kings, but from a very ancient lady, called 'Befana'. Experts think that her name is just another way of saying 'Epiphany' very quickly. Try it yourself, and see.

'The kings ride away in the snow and the rain. After 12 months we shall see them again.'

Old French rhyme, sung, with dancing, on 6th January.

'Deck the hall with boughs of holly,
Fa-la-la-la-la, la-la-la-la,
'Tis the season to be jolly,
Fa-la-la-la-la, la-la-la-la...'

New Year Carol; the English words were
written around 1880. The tune, originally for
dancing, is from Wales, and is
over 400 years old.

"It was the custom at Christmas for every
man's house, and also the parish Churches
[to be] decked with holm [holly], ivy, bays and
whatsoever the season of the year afforded to
be green..."

Stowe, Survey of London 1598

Chapter Seven

From mistletoe to fairy lights

Ho, ho, ho! Hello again! Good to see you! But what's that you're carrying? Armfuls of greenery... bulging carrier bags... trailing wires... and a TREE? Ah! I see! You've come to put up the Christmas decorations. But let me check the calendar first, before I let you in. I know that now, in the 21st century, Christmas decorations appear soon after Hallowe'en (31 October) or by December 1 at the latest. But I'm a traditionalist! Like people in the past, I only put up decorations on Christmas Eve.

Well, the date's okay, so come in, and make yourselves at home. Let's unpack your bags and see what you've brought with you. Hmmm – holly – and ivy – and mistletoe. Quite right! Well done! Though I've always thought it a bit peculiar that plants which are prickly, poisonous and parasitic[1] should be linked to such a festive time of year.

Green shoots

Santa's right; these are not very user-friendly plants – but they are all evergreen. They keep their leaves and bear fruit in the middle of winter, when most other vegetation is dead or dormant. To people living long ago, they appeared fresh and full of energy – a hopeful sign in a grim season.

Greek and Roman athletes wore crowns of laurel and bay, noble plants that stayed strong all year round. In Rome, at Saturnalia, houses and temples were decorated with evergreens. And Bacchus, the Roman god of wine, wore trailing wreaths of ivy in his hair.

1. *Holly is prickly and poisonous. Ivy is poisonous and clings, sinisterly… Mistletoe is poisonous and a parasite.*

In pagan Scandinavia, holly gave a home to wandering winter spirits. Its sharp spikes, hung at doors and windows, also kept them (and other evil-doers) safely out of the house. Tied to the bedpost, it sent sweet dreams.

According to English tradition, holly was manly: 'free [bold] and jolly', but ivy was female: 'loved and proved [trusted]'. If holly was brought indoors first on Christmas Eve, the man of the household was the master; if ivy, the housewife ruled! And mistletoe? Well, mistletoe was MAGIC:

"The druids... hold nothing more sacred than mistletoe... When they discover some, growing on an oak[1] tree, they gather it with great ceremony on the ninth day of the moon... They praise the moon, calling it 'healer of all', then prepare a ritual sacrifice and feast... they bring two white bulls... A priest dressed in white robes climbs the tree and cuts down the mistletoe, using a golden sickle. Onlookers catch it as it falls[2], in a white cloak. Then the bulls are sacrificed..."

Roman writer Pliny the Younger (AD 62–113)

1. A magic tree – mistletoe growing on it shared in its strength and healing powers.
2. Mistletoe loses this power if it touches the ground.

Peace and pleasure

According to Viking myths, Freya, goddess of love, ordered that mistletoe should grow half-way between earth and sky. When people walked under trees where it was, they kissed, to please her. Or else – if they were gruff, tough, hairy Viking warriors – they at least agreed to stop fighting for the day.

The Kissing Bunch

Ho, ho, ho! I like the look of this… Garlands like these Kissing Bunches (see facing page) have been made for hundreds of years, especially in northern England.

Yes! You CAN kiss the girls as they pass by. That's traditional! But each time you do so, you must remove one of the mistletoe berries. When they've all gone, the kissing has to stop!

DON'T, DON'T, DON'T eat the berries. They're VERY poisonous! And wash your hands thoroughly after touching them!

How to make a Kissing Bunch

1. Bend wire hoops into a globe shape, making a loop at the top.

2. Tie string or fix sticky tape around, to secure.

3. Attach leaves, tinsel, paper flowers and ribbons.

4. Finally, tie the mistletoe at the bottom.

A Kissing Bunch!

Sylvester

Kissing under the mistletoe was a peculiarly English tradition. But on New Year's Eve in Austria, there was a similar custom. A mysterious masked figure, an ugly old man, sat under a pine-tree branch in dark corners of country inns. He wore a wreath of mistletoe. When a pretty girl passed, he jumped up "and imprinted a rough kiss". When midnight struck, he was driven out into the snow to die (or pretend to), as a symbol of the Old Year.

Druid ceremonies, Viking pacts and other pre-Christian rituals scandalised early Church leaders, and led them to issue stern warnings:

"Let those people kindle lamps, who have no light [Christian faith]; let those for whom the fire [Hell!] lies in wait decorate doorposts with evergreens that will be burnt when their celebrations have ended. For them, these are suitable signs of darkness [damnation] and warnings of punishment. But you, Christians! You are a light for the world, and a tree that is always green [that is, you hope for everlasting life]. You have stopped going to pagan temples, so don't make your own front doors look like them!"

Tertullian (AD 160–220)

Few people listened. Today, almost 2000 years after those doom-laden threats thundered across the page, we still hang evergreen wreaths on our doors, and bunches of mistletoe from our ceilings. So what happened?

I think I can explain. Gentler – and maybe wiser – Church leaders decided, 'If you can't beat 'em, join 'em', and used ancient, pagan evergreens to send a new, Christian, message:

- Holly's sharp spikes symbolise the nails that crucified Jesus, and the cruel crown of thorns he was forced to wear. Its berries are red, like his blood.

- The holly-tree spread its spiky branches to hide baby Jesus from King Herod. In gratitude, Mary blessed the holly, and said it would stay green for ever.

- Ivy clings as it grows. In the same way, Christians must seek God.

- Mistletoe is a reminder of love and friendship – though traditionally, it's banned from most churches. Its pagan past is too powerful.

One plant, three names

The ancient Aztecs of Mexico used the bright red and green poinsettia plant to dye cloth, and as a medicine. Because its leaves have a leathery texture, they called it cuetlaxochitl (skin-flower). But around AD 1600, Christian missionaries in America gave it a new name: Noche Buena (the flower of Christmas Eve). And they told new stories about it. Details vary, but the tales all have the same theme:

"A young girl wanted to take a gift to Baby Jesus at Christmas, but she had no money. On her way to church, she picked a handful of weeds from the roadside; it was all she could find to offer. As she entered the church, the weeds were transformed into a beautiful red flower – a symbol of her love and good wishes."

Scientifically speaking, poinsettias are named after Joel Poinsett (d. 1851), US ambassador to Mexico and a keen botanist. He devoted many years to cultivating them.

- Instead of pagan 'crowns' or garlands, make an Advent wreath – a circle of greenery with candles. There can be up to 21 of these, but four or five are more usual: three royal purple, to symbolise Jesus, the 'Prince of Peace', one pink, to symbolise joy at his birthday, or else four blood-red ones, with perhaps a white one, for Jesus, in the middle.

Ahah! Some more greenery! Let's look at this tree you've brought! It seems a fine specimen! Where shall we hang it?

What do you mean? You don't hang it upside down from the ceiling? That was the usual custom – at least until around AD 1100. But we'll plant it in a pot, the modern way, if you prefer.

Hmmmmm. Looks more natural, I must admit. Now, how shall we decorate it? There are so many options! Let's take a trip down memory lane, to choose some…

A Christmas tree timeline...
with added decorations, of course!

c 380 *The first ever Christmas decoration?*
A Christian family in Rome decorates their secret tomb with a picture of Mary, Joseph and Baby Jesus in a stable in Bethlehem.

c 700 *The first Christmas trees? (1)*
Legends tell how St Boniface, a Christian missionary in Germany, saw pagans preparing to sacrifice a young boy at an oak tree. Furious, he chopped it down, and a holy evergreen sprouted in its place.

c 1200 (or earlier) *Winter Blossoms*
In Austria, cherry-tree twigs are brought indoors on St Barbara's Day (4th December). Kept in water in a warm place, they will bloom at Christmas.

Eating people...

No-one knows why little gingerbread biscuits shaped like people and animals are hung from Christmas trees. Perhaps they symbolise toys – or perhaps they remember the boy who Boniface saved, and other, less lucky, sacrifices?

1223 *Seeing is believing*

To help spread his Christmas message, St Francis of Assisi, Italy, organises the first presepe or 'crib' (re-enactment of Jesus's birth in Bethlehem). At first, the scene is played by real people – this continues in Italy until today, and inspires modern school Nativity Plays. Cribs using model people and animals also become a treasured Christmas tradition.

c 1400 (or earlier) *The first Christmas trees? (2)*
Pretty, holy 'Paradise Trees' come to family
homes (see box).

1501 *The first Chirstmas trees? (3)*
In Riga, Latvia, a decorated tree is spotted by
a mystified traveller. Perhaps it's a Paradise
Tree? Or perhaps it's a pine trunk, stripped of
bark, propped outside the door. That's an
ancient pagan Scandinavian custom.

From stage to sitting room

Religious plays – sometimes called Mystery
Plays – bring Bible stories to life in town
streets and in churches. Staged on 24
December, they celebrate the feast of Adam and
Eve. To represent the tree in Paradise from
which Eve took the 'apple of knowledge',
performers use an evergreen hung with apples
and other decorations, because real apple-tree
branches are bare in December.

1597 *We have the technology...*
Glass-worker Hans Greiner invents a method of making strings of glass beads. These are used as jewellery, or as decorations.

1605 *The first Christmas trees? (4)*
The first glimpse of Christmas trees as we know and love them today?

"At Christmas, they set up fir-trees in the parlours at Strasburg, and hang thereon roses cut out of many-coloured paper, apples, wafers, gold-foil, sweets etc..."

Anonymous writer, France.

c 1610 *All that glitters*
Tinsel is invented in Germany. At first it's made of real silver foil, cut into long thin strips. Later, it's made from (poisonous) lead or pewter. Originally used to drape holy statues, it gets the nickname 'Angels' Hair'. Soon, it's decorating trees.

c 1650 *'Childish' Christmas*

A Protestant minister complains about Christmas trees, hung with 'toys and sweets'. These remain in place until 6th January, then rowdy children overturn them, to 'rob' them of their treasures.

1670 *Sweet treats*

Choirboys at Cologne Cathedral, Germany, are given boiled-sugar sticks, bent to look like shepherds' crooks (see page 41). Before long, similar sticks are hung on Christmas trees.

1770 (or 1804 or 1816) *Across the Atlantic (1)*

German prisoners (or soldiers, or settlers – no-one knows for sure) put up the first Christmas trees in America. Some Americans call them 'a pagan mockery'.

c 1800 *Dangerous decorations*

Christmas pyramids of wood, paper and candles are made in Germany. They are cheaper than Christmas trees, but frighteningly easy to set on fire.

c 1820 *See the snow fall*

The first snow-globes are made in France, as paperweights. They are made of heavy, hollow glass, filled with water, tiny figures – and chips of bone!

c 1830 *Mathematical marvels*

Maths masters at a religious school in Herrnhut, Germany, accidentally invent a new Christmas decoration by making paper models to help pupils understand geometry. These 'Moravian Stars' are so pretty that they are hung up in homes, streets and churches. The largest have 110 points.

1832 *Perfect for a princess*

In England, Princess Victoria's trees (she had two) were decorated with sweets and candles. Presents were heaped underneath.

1824 *Tree tune*
Christmas trees are now so popular that songs are sung about them:

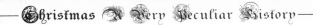

♪ "O Tannenbaum, o Tannenbaum, ♫
wie treu sind deine Blätter!
Du grünst nicht nur zur Sommerzeit,
nein auch im Winter, wenn es schneit."[1]

Ernst Anschutz, Germany

1847 *Across the Atlantic (2)*
First recorded use of candy canes to decorate a Christmas tree in America.

1847 *Glowing globes*
Hans Greiner, Germany, invents method of making coloured glass Christmas tree baubles. Each globe is individually blown into a mould. From the 1850s they are coated with silver nitrate on the inside, to make them reflective.

1. O Christmas tree, O Christmas tree
    How faithful (= long-lasting) are your needles!
    They grow green not only in summertime
    But in winter too, when it snows.

1854 *Tree topper*
It's now the fashion to decorate the very top of the tree:

"One branch had little nets of coloured paper... full of sugarplums... gold-painted apples and walnuts hung among other boughs... blue and white candles were balanced among the leaves... [plus]... at the very top, a big gold tinsel star..."

Hans Christian Andersen, Denmark

1859 *Make your own snow*
An American ladies' magazine publishes instructions for decorating Christmas branches with mock snow, made of cotton wool soaked in alum, which dries to a sparkly crystal finish.

1870s *The more the merrier*
Tree decorations get very extravagant.

"There was every kind of gilt hanging thing, from gilt pea-pods to butterflies on springs. There were shining flags and lanterns, and bird-cages, and nests with birds sitting on them, baskets of fruit, gilt apples, and bunches of grapes..."

Lucretia P Hale, USA

c 1870s *Window-shopping*
Macy's department store, New York, USA, pioneers special Christmas window displays – plus, soon after, the first in-store Santa Claus.

1882 *Electrifying!*
Edward H Johnson, of Edison Electric Light Company, USA, is the first to decorate his tree with electric light bulbs. There are 80 of them, and their colours are patriotic, if not very Christmassy: red, white and blue.

c 1880 *Fake finery*
Artificial Christmas trees are made in Germany, using long, fluffy feathers, often dyed green, fixed to a wire frame.

1904 *Lighting-up*
Christmas lights – not yet electric – are first used to decorate outdoor Christmas trees, USA.

1910 *Mass Market*
By now, over 1000 Woolworth stores in the USA sell German and USA-made Christmas tree decorations.

c 1920 *Up in flames*
Tinsel is now made of paper covered with aluminium foil. It catches fire very quickly.

1927 *Outdoor extravaganza*
First organised outdoor Christmas light displays, called 'Festivals of Lights', USA.

1930 *Brushed off!*
The Addis Brush Company – famous for making brushes to clean toilets – uses the same technology to manufacture artificial Christmas trees.

1956 *Switched on*
First electric lights on outdoor Christmas trees, in the USA. Soon, Christmas lights are everywhere…

c1960 *Plastic attack*
Christmas trees, holly, ivy and tinsel are now all made from plastic.

c 2000 *HOW many?*
Around 35 million natural Christmas trees are sold in the USA every year.

2008 *Risky glitter*
Local council in England bans school crossing worker from decorating his 'lollipop' STOP sign with Christmas tinsel, for health and safety reasons.

2009 *Christmas crisis – in China*

Over half the world's Christmas decorations are now made in just one manufacturing district of China. It faces crisis as trade slumps in the global recession.

Home fires burning

In 2009, the US Fire Prevention Authority published statistics for 2003–2007:

- Fire-fighters were called out to around 250 Christmas tree fires every year.

- The fires caused, on average, 14 deaths and 26 injuries per year, plus $13.8 million damage to property.

*"England was Merry England when
Old Christmas[1] brought his sports again"*

*Strangely, a Scot[2], not an English
person, wrote that. But he was right.
Traditionally (except in Scotland), Christmas was
always celebrated with music, dancing, plays and
party games – the rowdier the better!*

Round and round

What would Christmas be like without carols?
The first carols were round dances,
accompanied by folk songs, for any festival
celebration. But, as Christianity spread
through Europe, old pagan lyrics were
replaced by Christian words. At least 500
carols composed before AD 1500 have
survived; many more have probably
disappeared. Why?

- After c 1500, religious reformers replaced
  carols and dancing with new 'godly and sober'
  hymns.

- After c 1600, Puritans preferred chanting
  psalms.

1. Father Christmas
2. novelist Sir Walter Scott (1771–1832)

162

- By the 1700s, many old carols had been forgotten. Religious revivalists (for example, in England, the Wesley brothers, leaders of the Methodist movement) penned new Christmas hymns – most famously, 'Hark the Herald Angels Sing' (first version 1739).

- In the 1800s, Victorian writers joined Charles Dickens and the royal family (see page 170) in making Christmas a time for children. Most of today's popular carols were written then, for example

:
    1848 Once in Royal David's City
    1857 We Three Kings of Orient Are
    1868 O Little Town of Bethlehem
    1885 Away in A Manger

Dangerous games

When you were tired of singing and dancing, how else could you have fun at Christmas? By playing parlour games – the oldest, such as boistrous 'Blind Man's Buff' might have originated as ways of choosing victims for Yuletide sacrifice. Many others (such as 'Hunt the Slipper') involved searching and finding, some also demanded forfeits.

Most games were noisy; but some, such as 'Bullet Pudding' (retreiving a bullet from a bowl of flour using lips and nose only), were extremely messy – especially if you sneezed! A few were downright dangerous. Players of 'Snapdragon' tried to snatch raisins that had been soaked in brandy and then set on fire.

Oh yes it is...

By the 1700s, play-acting was popular among amateurs and professionals. As well as charades, party-goers might play 'Characters': each person drew lots to see which strange or fantastic character (often masked and in disguise) they had to be for the whole evening. Around the same time, Pantomime – which originated in ancient Rome – arrived in England, and became the most popular children's Christmas entertainment. The old Roman myths and battle-stories were replaced by favourite folk-tales, and Roman masked actors and dancers were transformed into Principal Boys (always played by attractive young women) and Pantomime Dames (always acted by comic old men).

Instant tradition

- **1742, Dublin, Ireland**: First performance of German-born, London-resident, G.F. Handel's 'Messiah': 'a sort of 18th century musical' – but originally written for Easter. By the mid 1800s, it becomes vastly popular, with pre-Christmas recitals by massed choirs and orchestras of over 3000 performers attracting audiences of 10,000 and more.

- **1818, near Salzburg, Austria**: Junior priest Joseph Mohr and schoolteacher Franz Gruber are the first to sing what will soon be the world's most famous Austrian song. No, not 'The Sound of Music', but the Christmas carol 'Silent Night'. Mohr wrote the words; Gruber composed a guitar accompaniment after the local church organ broke down. Since then, Silent Night has been translated into over 300 different languages and dialects.

- **1880, Truro, SW England**: In a wooden shed, the local Bishop holds the first-ever service of 'Nine Lessons [Bible readings] and Carols'. In 1918, his idea is copied at King's College, Cambridge, home of a world-famous choir. The service is first broadcast in 1928 and has been ever since, except for just one year (1930).

'The picturesque ceremonies and rude[1] festivities that distinguished the Christmas of bygone times have passed away, and, for ourselves, we can regard the loss of them without regret. We are too thankful to have lighted upon[2] a more civilized age ...'

British printer and publisher
Henry Vitazelly (1820–1894)

*"Christmas is a good time:
a kind, forgiving, charitable, pleasant time..."*

"It is good to be children sometimes, and never better than at Christmas, when its mighty Founder was a child Himself."

Girl in 'A Christmas Carol' by
English novelist Charles Dickens
(1812–1870)

*"Christmas won't be Christmas
without any presents!"*

From 'Little Women', by American novelist
Louisa May Alcott (1832–1888)

1. rough
2. arrived at

Chapter Eight

Victorian Christmas

or once, I'm not laughing or saying 'Ho, ho, ho!'. Come with me to the 19th century, and I'll show you why. Christmas has become more complicated. Delightful for some — but dreadful for others.

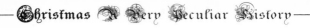

All change!

In 1819, American traveller Washington Irving enthusiastically reported: "Christmas is still a period of delightful excitement in England…" The Christmas traditions he was praising were hundreds of years old. But Britain was changing – and quickly. There were new mines and factories, new railways, new machines and new cities – with serious social problems. From 1837, there was also a new young queen, Victoria, who reigned until 1901. Along with all these changes, Christmas was changing, too.

A new kind of Christmas

As millions of workers left farming villages to live in cities and towns, old country traditions, such as the Yule Log and wassailing, became impossible to continue. Now, celebrations focused on individual families, rather than whole communities. Christmas became 'a time for children', rather than for adults. Parents gave more gifts to their youngsters than to their friends or to people who worked for them.

Consumer Christmas

Christmas also became a time for selling and consuming. Instead of old-style, simple, home-made gifts and decorations, new shops offered the latest Christmas luxuries. Families were tempted to buy these – and then felt guilty or anxious for spending so much money. At the same time, new mass media – cheap newspapers, novels and advertisements – created a new, sentimental, image of the 'ideal' Merry Christmas, which few real-life families could achieve – and many could not afford.

Christmas critic

In 1843, British novelist Charles Dickens wrote what quickly became the world's best-known Christmas story. Called 'A Christmas Carol', it tells how money-lender Ebenezer Scrooge – a "squeezing, wrenching, grasping, scraping, clutching, covetous, old sinner" – is visited by ghosts on Christmas Eve. They show him how so many poor people suffer at Christmas, and encourage him to help them. At the same time, the ghosts show Scrooge just how happy an ideal Victorian Christmas could be.

Dickens's 'A Christmas Carol' was fiction, not fact. But his descriptions of happy family gatherings made such an impact that he has been called 'the man who invented Christmas'. Victorian readers tried to copy the image of the Christmas he created.

"Christmas? Bah! Humbug!"

Ebenezer Scrooge in
Charles Dickens's
A Christmas Carol

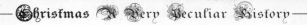
A time for giving?

The growing gap between rich and poor meant that children and old people might starve to death at Christmas, while rich families feasted nearby. Charities did their best to help, but they could not cope – and often treated the poor very harshly. In fact, some Victorians believed that the poor were to blame for their own misfortunes. They had no right to be happy at Christmas.

So! Victorian Christmases were not always cosy and cheerful. And sometimes they seem surprisingly modern. Readers! Do you know how many of today's Christmas 'traditions' were newly invented by the Victorians?

• A day off work?

Until around 1830, businesses closed for about 30 holy days each year. But Victorian factories could not stand idle for so long, and, in 1834, all holidays except four were abolished. Christmas Day survived, but many servants and labourers still had to work – not least to prepare Christmas celebrations for their employers. Others were given time off – with pay – only very reluctantly:

> "[Christmas is] A poor excuse for picking a man's pocket every twenty-fifth of December! ... But I suppose you must have the whole day [off]. Be here all the earlier next morning."
>
> Scrooge, in Charles Dickens's
> *A Christmas Carol*

• Coming home for Christmas?

Rich? Victorians travelled by horse-drawn coach or carriage, or by first-class train.

Poor? Victorians still made the effort. How far can you walk in a day? Or ride on a farm cart? Perhaps you can afford third-class rail travel;

it's bumpy and draughty, but fast. In cities, there are new, cheap, horse-drawn trams and omnibuses.

• Huge Christmas dinner?

The Victorians feasted on Christmas Day, in the afternoon or evening (Queen Victoria's dinner began late, at 9pm). In the 1830s they ate goose or beef. But by around 1900, turkey was the favourite. Everyone also loved boiled Christmas pudding: "like a speckled cannon ball, so hard and firm, blazing [with lighted brandy]… with Christmas holly stuck on top". Queen Victoria's cooks made over 200 puddings, and handed them out as royal presents.

• Visiting rleatives, and being visited?

Of course! This was essential!

> *"…all the children of the house were running out into the snow to meet their married sisters, brothers, cousins, uncles, aunts, and be the first to greet them."*
>
> Charles Dickens's *A Christmas Carol*

• Office parties?

Oh yes! Usually on Christmas Eve. Here's a dance in a company warehouse:

"In came Mrs Fezziwig [the boss's wife], one vast substantial smile. In came the three Miss Fezziwigs, beaming and lovable. In came the six young followers [sweethearts] whose hearts they broke. In came all the young men and women employed in the business...

In they all came, one after another; some shyly, some boldly, some gracefully, some awkwardly, some pushing, some pulling... Away they all went [started dancing], twenty couple at once... round and round..."

Charles Dickens's *A Christmas Carol*

• Christmas cards?

By 1800, rich families, and business or professional people, sent Christmas letters, wishing friends the 'compliments of the season'. Writing these took a lot of time. So, in 1843, London businessman Henry Cole paid an artist to design ready-printed cards, instead. He sent them by the new, cheap, British postal service, which he helped organise in 1840.

At first, Christmas cards were expensive, but fast new printing machines soon made them cheaper. By 1880, over 11 million were sold in the UK every year.

Red, red robin

The first Christmas card had a picture of – guess what?! – a happy Victorian family feasting, though it also showed them handing out food and clothes to beggars. But other Christmas symbols soon appeared on cards, together with robins. Why? Robins have red chest-feathers, and reminded Victorians of the postal workers who delivered their cards. They wore red jackets, and, like robins, were nicknamed 'redbreasts'.

• Christmas crackers?

BANG! What's that? The latest Christmas invention: crackers! Inspired by French bon-bons (sugared almonds in twisted paper wrappers), they were invented by Tom Smith, a London sweet-maker, in 1847. Trying to find new ways to sell his products, he wrapped them, added mottoes, small gifts – and (after he'd been startled by his crackling log fire) little strips of chemical explosive.

• Christmas advertising?

Keen to win more Christmas customers? Use new technology – cheaper colour printing – and hand out 'trade cards' with bright Christmas scenes and cheery advertising slogans. Or else fill your shop windows with eye-catching displays. You might even like to stay open for late-night shopping, like Macy's department store in New York City, which pioneered this way to increase Christmas sales in 1867.

• The latest factory-made toys?

What did Santa – or Papa – bring to lucky Victorian boys and girls? New, fashionable china dolls, metal soldiers, and fluffy stuffed animals (made in bulk by the Steiff company in Germany from 1880). Around the same time, new precision cutting machines made jigsaw puzzles cheap – and popular.

• Cards and board games?

They say that children's toys reflect adult society. Well, that was certainly true of two new board games. American 'Moneta, or Money Makes Money' (1888) must have appealed to young entrepreneurs. So, perhaps, did Snakes and Ladders (1870): all about risk, success – or failure. And the most popular new Victorian card game? 'Happy Families' (invented around 1850), of course!

• Family gathered around a glowing screen?

No, not the TV or DVD player, but a Magic Lantern show: coloured pictures painted on glass slides, projected using bright light onto a cloth screen. Travelling showmen gave public performances; rich families watched their own Magic Lanterns at home.

"We attended divine service in the Chapel of Prahia [New Zealand]; part of the service being read in English, and part in the native language... we did not hear of any recent acts of cannibalism; but Mr Stokes found burnt human bones strewed round a fire-place on a small island ..."

Charles Darwin, Beagle Diaries, 1835

"Each nation, naturally, has fashioned its own Christmas. The English have made it a season of solid material comfort, of good fellowship and 'charity', with a slight flavour of soothing religion..."

British historian Clement A Miles, 1912

'The War on Christmas: How the Liberal Plot to Ban the Sacred Christian Holiday is Worse Than You Thought.'

Book title, USA, 2007.

Chapter Nine

Still a special day?

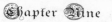

Ho, ho, ho! Today, Christmas is the world's favourite holiday, celebrated by people of many different faiths — and none — all around the world. It's fun. It's expensive. It's sometimes even dangerous! But is it still special?

One very special Christmas

Between 1914 and 1918, European nations and their allies worldwide fought 'the war to end all wars'. It brought death and suffering on a new and terrible scale. But, even in the middle of appalling bloodshed, Christmas time promised peace, for a while, to soldiers on both sides. Brief Christmas truces were arranged; the most famous was at Christmas 1914, when Allied and German troops exchanged gifts of food and souvenirs, and sang carols to each other. They were ordered to start killing again at New Year.

Christmas goes global

On 25 December 1549, Jesuit priests celebrated the first ever Christmas in Japan. The same day, in 1620, newly-arrived Mayflower colonists shivered in a 'hideous and desolate wilderness' on the east coast of America. In 1643, again at Christmas, a British trading ship sailed past a rocky speck of land in the vast Pacific Ocean, half a world away from home.

Today, Christmas Island (as the sailors named it) houses a controversial Australian immigration detention centre, but, almost everywhere else, the name and concept of Christmas have been linked much more cheerfully with local customs and ideas. Some of the resulting celebrations would certainly have startled Yuletide revellers and early Christians, almost 2000 years ago.

Come with me on a whistle-stop world tour, to see just some of the sights!

Australia: The world's biggest open-air carol concerts, with over 100,000 singers. Christmas barbecues on the beach, plus Santa in a fluffy white beard – and red swimming trunks.

USA: Classic Christmas movies: 'It's a Wonderful Life (1946); 'White Christmas' (1954); 'Rudolph the Red Nosed Reindeer' (1964); 'Elf' (2003). Memorable Christmas songs, from Eartha Kitt's seductive 'Santa Baby' (1953) to the all-time best-selling Christmas novelty number: 'Grandma Got Run Over by a Reindeer' (1979). Also: drive-in Christmas cribs, 'Happy Holidays' greetings, and a new midwinter festival, Kwanzaa, created by African-Americans during the Civil Rights movement of the 1960s.

UK: Massive displays of 'house-bling'. In 2004, a home covered in 20,000 lights causes traffic disruption, complaints from neighbours, 'increased crime' – and costs over £7,000 to police. TV specials and charity records: Band Aid's 'Do they Know it's Christmas?' sells 1.25 million copies in just seven days in 1984. Plus a world record for sending Christmas cards: 641 million in 2007.

British Commonwealth: 'My husband and I…' HM Queen Elizabeth continues the Royal Christmas Broadcast tradition started by her grandfather George V in 1932, moving from radio to TV in 1957.

Japan: Christmas cakes made of whipped cream and strawberries, Christmas Eve dinners in romantic 'love hotels', presents, presents, presents – and the Virgin Mary riding a broomstick, on greetings cards.

Africa: A time for new clothes and big, big family gatherings – with, if possible, roast goat or beef, or chicken stew, to share. Children sing carols and dance in the streets; Christian families go to church. In Ethiopia, men play 'Ganna', a fast, traditional ball game, like hockey.

Bosnia: Father Christmas is banned for being alien to local Muslim tradition, 2008.

China: 'Trees of Light' are draped with paper garlands. Children hang up gauze stockings for gifts from Dun Ce Lao Ren (Grandfather Christmas). Streets are decorated with dazzling lights; shops display tempting gifts – and dress staff in Santa hats.

India: A national holiday, even though most Indians are not Christians. Families decorate their homes with mango leaves, Nativity scenes and little oil-burning lamps. Santa visits big city stores, and streets are brightly-decorated.

Israel and Palestinian Territories: It's the peak tourist season (around 60,000 Christmas visitors) in the lands where Jesus was born. In Israel, it's also the holy time of Hanukkah, festival of lights.

Wealthy nations worldwide: Christmas comes full circle – from a Victorian one-day holiday back to the old Twelve Days of Christmas, or more. Businesses close between Christmas Eve and New Year's Day, while privileged families jet round the world in search of rest and relaxation. Their favourite destinations? Snowy ski-slopes, ice-hotels in the Arctic, or balmy tropical beaches.

Strange but true....

- On average, each British person ate 27 mince pies over Christmas 2008, and 14 brussels sprouts.

- 3.5 million people went online shopping on Christmas Day 2007.

- 45% of British adults worried about spending too much money at Christmas 2009.

- It is claimed that 31 people have died since 1996 through watering their Christmas trees while the lights were still switched on.

- Seven out of every ten British dogs are given Christmas presents.

- British businesses sold 2 tonnes of crackers and party hats overseas in 2009.

- Britons throw away around 83 square miles of wrapping paper each Christmas.

- Christmas Roses, which bloom at midwinter, are so poisonous (they cause terrible diarrhoea) that they were used as a chemical weapon by ancient Greek armies.

- On average, each British person gains 2kg over the Christmas holidays – and around 80,000 attend hospital accident and emergency departments.

In AD 1012, a German priest was leading prayers in his church on Christmas Eve. But he was disturbed by 'a company of young men and maids' singing and dancing in the churchyard outside. He asked them to be quiet, but they refused. So he prayed some more, and the revellers found that they could not stop – for a whole year! Life is very different today, but Christmas is still much the same as it was 1000 years ago: for some, a religious festival; for others, a time for energetic midwinter merry-making.

For many people, however, Christmas is a lot of things, all jumbled together. It's a blend of pagan feasting and dancing, Christian faith and hope, (rather limited) community sharing and giving, licensed misbehaviour, sport and sacred music, family togetherness (and quarrels), sweet sentiment, hypocrisy and simple childlike joy – all mixed with modern marketing and crass consumerism.

But whatever your Christmas is, we wish you 'Peace on Earth, and Goodwill...' That's the best Christmas present anyone could hope for!

Glossary

Advent The Christian holy season before Christmas; a time of hopeful waiting and showing sorrow for sins.

Auld Lang Syne 'Times Long Ago'; title of a poem celebrating friendship by Scot Robert Burns (d. 1796), often sung on New Year's Eve.

axis (of the Earth) An imaginary line through the Earth's centre, linking the North Pole and the South Pole.

boar Male pig. Wild boars are huge and fierce – and were a favourite food at Christmas.

botanist Scientist who studies plants.

Bûche de Noel Christmas Log (a cake or dessert)

census Population count

disciples Followers of a religious leader.

dormant Sleeping or (of plants) temporarily non-active.

druids Celtic 'wise men'.

Eastern Christians Followers of Jesus Christ in Russia, Eastern Europe, Armenia and nearby lands.

epiphany Appearance of God on Earth

flagon Bottle-shaped jug.

gospel Books in the Bible telling the story of Jesus's life.

grove Clump of trees.

guisers Singers and dancers in disguise. Often, they begged from door to door.

Hanukkah Jewish winter festival of light, when candles are lit and gifts are given.

infusion Flavoured liquid produced by soaking a substance in water.

kindle To set fire to.

Kwanzaa Midwinter festival, created by African-Americans during the Civil Rights movement of the 1960s. It celebrates family, community and African heritage.

Lord of Misrule Person chosen to lead the festivities during the Twelve Days of Christmas.

mummers Actors and dancers in masks and elaborate costumes.

pagans Followers of ancient, pre-Christian religions.

prophet Messenger from God.

Puritans People with strict Protestant beliefs, active in the 16th and 17th centuries.

quince Fruit similar to an apple, with a sweet, enticing scent.

revelation Idea or message sent by God.

Saturnalia Roman midwinter festival.

Solstice Times (midsummer and midwinter) when the Sun appears to be highest and lowest in the sky.

waits Carol-singers; originally night-watchmen, later poor children.

wassail Ancient ceremony that aimed to bring fertility to apple trees.

Index

Ancient Egypt
A Very Peculiar History
The Art of Embalming:
Mummy Myth and Magic
With added Squishy Bits
Jim Pipe
ISBN: 978-1-906714-92-5

Brighton
A Very Peculiar History
With added Hove, actually
David Arscott
ISBN: 978-1-906714-89-5

Ireland
A Very Peculiar History
With NO added Blarney
Jim Pipe
ISBN: 978-1-905638-98-7

Rations
A Very Peculiar History
With NO added Butter
David Arscott
ISBN: 978-1-907184-25-3

London
A Very Peculiar History
With added Jellied Eels
Jim Pipe
ISBN: 978-1-907184-26-0

Vampires
A Very Peculiar History
With added Bite
Fiona Macdonald
ISBN: 978-1-907184-39-0

Scotland
A Very Peculiar History
With NO added Haggis
or Bagpipes
Fiona Macdonald

**Vol. 1: From ancient times
to Robert the Bruce**
ISBN: 978-1-906370-91-6

**Vol. 2: From the Stewarts
to modern Scotland**
ISBN: 978-1-906714-79-6

The Blitz
A Very Peculiar History
With NO added Doodlebugs
David Arscott
ISBN: 978-1-907184-18-5

Wales
A Very Peculiar History
With NO added Laverbread
Rupert Matthews
ISBN: 978-1-907184-19-2

The World Cup
A Very Peculiar History
With NO added Time
David Arscott
ISBN: 978-1-907184-38-3

Castles
A Very Peculiar History
With added dungeons
Jacqueline Morley
ISBN: 978-1-907184-48-2

Heroes, Gods and Monsters of
Ancient Greek Mythology
Michael Ford
ISBN: 978-1-906370-92-3

Heroes, Gods and Monsters of
Celtic Mythology
Fiona Macdonald
ISBN: 978-1-905638-97-0

Wishing You a Merry Christmas.
May Father Christmas fill
Your Stocking.